WHY ME?

Overcome Life's Battles and Soldier On

WHY ME?

Overcome Life's Battles and Soldier On

MISTY MICHAEL

Clovercroft Publishing

Why Me? Overcome Life's Battles and Soldier On

© 2015 by Misty Michael

Published by Clovercroft Publishing, Franklin, Tennessee

Published in association with Larry Carpenter of Christian Book Services, LLC.
www.christianbookservices.com

Cover Design by Doug White

Interior Design by Suzanne Lawing

Edited by Tammy Kling and Gail Fallen

Printed in the United States of America

978-1-942557-28-9

WHAT PEOPLE ARE SAYING ABOUT *WHY ME?*

"This book reveals a journey that many in today's culture can relate to. The writer illustrates a tremendous level of endurance in tough times. It gives a guiding voice to those who are going through, or have gone through similar times. Look for the courage, strength, answers, and hope. I highly recommend this book!"
—D. G. HARGROVE, SENIOR PASTOR,
NORTH CITIES, GARLAND, TEXAS

"The tentacles of abuse are pervasive and far reaching in the lives of those who have been sexually abused, yet the love of God reaches further and deeper. In *Why Me?* we are given a picture of both. We are able to see the pain, the confusion, the shame, and the reality of the impact of being sexually abused. We are also privileged to see the greater impact of prayer, God's love, mercy, and grace. Misty Michael's story is sadly similar to many, yet still unique. Her story is one that portrays hope and empowers those who have been victimized with realistic, practical, and sound insight. Her story is encapsulated in Romans 8:37-38: 'No, in all these things we are more than conquerors through him who loved us. For I am convinced that neither death nor life, neither angels nor demons, neither the present nor the future, nor any powers, neither height nor depth, nor anything else in all creation, will be able to separate us from the love of God that is in Christ Jesus our Lord.' *Why Me?* provides the hope and encouragement that is necessary on the road to wholeness and which is found in God's healing and restorative power."
—DOLORES A. GUILLIOD, MA, LPC

"Misty's story is riveting, as is the style in which she tells it. At times I cried while reading it. I also rejoiced. But it is the principles she shares that make it a life-altering book. If you have experienced brokenness and are trying to find your way, or perhaps wanting to help others find theirs—if you have ever asked 'why *me*?'—this book may offer the answers you are looking for."
—DR. EUGENE T. WILSON, AUTHOR AND
FOUNDER OF EQUIPPING LEADERS

"Like Job of old, when we suffer, we often ask God despairing questions like, why me? But in Misty Michael's work, she turns this question on its head to reveal the mystery of how God turns the "why me?" of despair into a question of wonder at how an infinite God uses our pain for His purpose.
—ROBERT RAAB, MENTAL HEALTH PROFESSIONAL
AND PSYCHOLOGY INSTRUCTOR AT
INDIANA WESLEYAN UNIVERSITY

I dedicate this book to my husband, Ken, who has taught me what true love is all about. Your strength, patience, and encouragement have been invaluable throughout my healing process. Thank you for loving me through all of my growing pains.

Thank you for giving me room to grow and encouraging me to never give up on myself or the calling of God on my life. Thank you for praying with me about this project and all of your hard work. This book is as much yours as it is mine, and I thank God He gave me you, My Prince Charming. I love you.

ACKNOWLEDGMENTS

Thank you . . .

Justin Michael, for all of the effort and heart you put into this book. The song you wrote for this book, "Why Me," is God inspired, and I know it will bless many. You bless and inspire me every day as I witness firsthand your passion for the kingdom of God. May God continually bless and enlarge your territory. I love you.

McKinley Michael, "Mommy's Little Princess," for all of the little hugs and the thumbs up while I finished this book. I truly believe you are my biggest fan. I love you more than life.

Pastor D. G. and Rebecca Hargrove, for the love, wisdom, and encouragement I have received from you over the last decade. Thank you for believing in me and helping me build the ministry God has called me to. I have learned so much under your leadership.

Rev. Johnny and Nancy Hargrove, for the friendship and love you have shown to my family and me. Your prayers and spiritual guidance have been invaluable. You have a heart for the kingdom of God and a true love for His people.

Rev. Bobby and Glenda Stanley, for playing such a vital role in my healing process. I wouldn't be where I am today without your guidance. Thank you for believing in me and pouring into my life. I truly feel I am a better person because of your influence.

To the countless others who have prayed with me and given me your feedback on this book, I am grateful.

CONTENTS

PART 1: INTRODUCTION

Loneliness. Hopelessness. Worthlessness. Addiction. Abuse. Have you ever found yourself there? Trapped in this cycle with no seeming way of escape? No light at the end of your long, dark, and empty tunnel? Wondering if your very existence even mattered, buckling under the pressure of pain, crying out to anything or anyone that can hear, "Why me"? If so, this book is for you.

Why Me? is a story of God's immeasurable grace and bountiful mercy. This book will set you upon a journey to walk through my life's battles. I will share with you, through my own experiences, how God took a girl who was lost, broken, and hopeless on a path of self-destruction and set her on a pathway of victorious living. I will expose the very real and dark struggles that I have endured. We will walk through the ups and the downs of my abuse, addiction, and failures. You will see a girl—destitute, broken and empty—receive hope, healing, and purpose through the love of God.

The reason for this book is simple: it's YOU. Through my life's experiences and the countless battles endured along my journey, I believe God has given me insight to help you heal. Together with God, you will see that there is a way out. If you find yourself at battle, in the middle of a life crisis, this book will minister to you. No matter how dark your night might be, no matter how hopeless your life situation may seem, join hands with this book and set yourself upon a journey from your broken path to a path of healing and liberty in the Lord. You can survive life's battles and live victoriously. I want you to understand that you are not alone, and there is HOPE.

This book is based upon a true story. Some of the names have been altered to protect the identity of those in the story who are still living and have found healing and forgiveness in Christ Jesus.

1

FACE-TO-FACE WITH MY ENEMY

"Just one more time," I thought, holding out my arm, waiting for my love to shoot me up again. He hated to do it, but I begged and begged every time until he gave in. All I wanted was that first cool, sweet rush, like I had never done it before, but would do over and over again. It was mind blowing. As he pushed the needle into my arm and drained the syringe of cocaine into my veins, I knew it was going to be good. The taste of the cocaine in my mouth was strong. It was then, at the very moment the taste became stronger than ever before, I knew I had mixed it too strong. Something wasn't right.

I felt different, deathly sick to my stomach, and riddled with fear. As I stood in front of the sink at a local motel room, looking at myself in the mirror, gasping for breath, trying to take the inhale that wasn't coming, I felt my heart begin to drum wildly and then stop. Panic began to set in as I grabbed Jim's arm and tried to talk, but the words would not come. He immediately knew something was wrong, and the fear in his eyes said more than a thousand words could ever say. I then turned back to the mirror, made eye contact with myself, and grabbed the sink with a death grip. But I grew faint.

Thoughts began to flood my mind as reality set in. I thought, *This could be it. I am going to die. I am going to hell.* It is amazing how, in such a short amount of time, that every sermon you heard preached, every word your mother spoke, the cries of repentance, and the promises you continually make to God can all converge simultaneously in a way that oddly makes sense. While all of this echoed in my mind, Jim turned on the faucet and began splashing cold water on my face. I remember, in my mind, screaming out the name: *Jesus, Jesus, Jesus.* About the time I gasped for breath, all I could hear was the name of Jesus being repeated faintly over and over again and the sound of running water. I felt weak, ready to cave in, and then he grabbed me and helped me to a seat on the commode in the bathroom. I remember trying to scream but could only weakly say, "Turn off the water." My ears were so sensitive to sound that it felt as though I were standing at the bottom of Niagara Falls.

I can't describe it any other way than to say my whole body felt numb. My legs were numb; it was hard to walk. I asked him to help me to the bed to lie down, and he picked me up and gently carried me to the bed. All I kept saying was, "I feel bad, real bad. I don't want to die."

Although I could breathe, I was not convinced I was going to live. I was scared to close my eyes, in fear I would not wake up. My heart leaped up and down erratically, but I felt lifeless. I began to sob and think, *What have I done to my life?* Most everyone thought I had it made. My life was perfect. How easy it is to fool those who think they know you. On the perimeter I can see where it looked as though I had it all together, but inside I was living a lie. I remember lying on the bed of a cheap motel room, curled up in a ball sobbing and praying, as I held onto a pillow for dear life. I was scared. I begin to cry out to God, "Why me? If I'm going to die lost and go to a devil's hell, why did you raise me from the dead? Why did you give me life when I died as a baby, so small and helpless? And why, please tell me, *why* did you give me life in this very moment when I'm at my lowest and most unworthy of your love?"

2

A PATH OF
SELF-DESTRUCTION

Funny how quickly life can go from having a good time, doing what feels good, to a reality check, all in such a short span of time. As I laid there sobbing, trying to figure out the mess I had made of my life, I quickly began to realize that the choices I had made in an effort to find acceptance and love were leading me down a path going nowhere quickly. I began reasoning, desperately trying to figure out how I got here. Right here. This very moment.

My mind immediately raced back to the story I had heard growing up from my parents, grandparents, and saints in the church.

One Sunday evening when I was about eighteen months old, my family was at church, enjoying the presence of God. This particular evening, my mother, Jerrie, was holding me in her arms when I became very ill. They had just finished the worship service as the last song had been sung and the pastor, Joseph Todd, took the pulpit to preach. As he began reading a portion of Scripture from where he planned to preach, I began to get fretful. The pastor's wife, Sister Todd, asked my mother if I was okay. My mother told her no, that my cheeks were flushed and I was burning hot with a fever. My mother knew that something was wrong, but did not quite know the severity. Sister Todd told my mother to go have me prayed for, but since pastor was getting ready to preach, my mother thought she would wait a minute. Then, as I lay in my mother's arms, my body fell limp. My head and heels hung as to make a perfect circle. Without another thought about interrupting the service, my mom and dad jumped up and ran to the front of the church to have the pastor pray for me. As my grandmother Lula and Sister Todd saw my limp body, they ran to the front, joining my parents, and began to pray, sensing the urgency of the moment.

Of course you can only imagine my parents' helplessness and the fear that raced through their hearts as they realized something was wrong with their baby girl. By this time the situation had become chaotic; the whole church began to realize something was wrong and came flooding around us. The pastor stopped preaching and came down to the front where my parents were. He took my lifeless body into his arms and began to pray the prayer of faith for God's mercy. At this time the church had gathered around the altar where my limp body was and began praying intensely for a miracle. During this time, my big blue eyes had become fixed in my head and were not moving or blinking. Breath had left my body. There was no pulse. They knew that nothing short of a miracle would bring me back. I had died.

I can just hear the cries of desperation that poured out of the hearts of my parents, grandparents, and church family as reality was setting in that I was gone. Brother Todd was a man of prayer and the church was a praying church, so as you can imagine, they laid me on that altar and began to pray for a miracle. After several minutes had passed, which seemed like an eternity to my parents and others who prayed, they said I just sat up on the altar and looked around like, "Why are all you people gathered around me, crying and praying?" My parents grabbed me in their arms and held me and praised God with a thankful heart, as He just gave them their little girl again for the second time. Everyone was amazed, as I didn't act like anything was wrong with me. My fever was gone. My mother, of course, took me to the doctor to find out what happened, and the doctor looked at my mom as if to say, "Why are you bringing a well baby to see me. She is fine."

God had performed His first miracle in my life. The verse that has been etched in my mind is Ephesians 1:11–12, "In him we were also chosen, having been predestined according to the plan of him who works out everything in conformity with the purpose of his will, in order that we, who were the first to hope in Christ, might be for the praise of his glory."

Oftentimes I thought, *If God is love, why do I feel all of this pain?* I grew up on a church pew. I experienced the power of God. I knew what it was like to experience a genuine move of God's Spirit. My life growing up was pretty good, with a few exceptions. God blessed me to be raised in a family where I was loved and didn't want for much. I did not grow up rich by any stretch of the imagination, but my parents worked hard to see that my brother and I didn't have to experience poverty as they did growing up. They wanted us to have more. My parents went to church regularly and were heavily involved in the ministry of that local assembly. I do not recall a lot of my childhood, but I do remember the incident that changed the course of direction for my family.

My mother was deeply wounded by someone in the ministry and never fully recovered. I remember as a small child watching my mom try to make amends with the one who hurt her, and even in an attempt to do the right thing, complete healing never occurred; the wound never healed. The Devil began to use this one event to unravel the life of a wonderful lady. It started with missing a service here and a service there until a month went by. Then the feelings of guilt and shame set in, which made it harder for her to go back. Shortly after my mother stopped attending church, my dad stopped going to worship as well. It seemed that in a moment of time our priorities as a family changed.

Do not underestimate the power of being offended. If left alone and not given to God, it WILL destroy you. The sad part is, Satan doesn't just want you. He wants the generations that come after you as well.

I had praying grandparents, thank God, who saw to it that I never missed a church service. I loved church. One Sunday evening while everyone was at the altar, I felt the urge to go pray. I wanted to receive the Spirit of God. I watched others receive it, and I wanted to experience it for myself. I remember walking to the altar and kneeling down to pray. Before I knew it, I was standing to my feet, praising the Lord as others were praying with me, and God filled me with the wonderful gift of the Holy Ghost at age six. My granny made it her mission to make sure I was at every service, youth activity, and anything else the church provided that I could be involved in. She realized if I was going to be saved, she must instill something in me, and that she did. Granny Lulu was my spiritual rock.

Around the age of seven, I began to be subjected to sexual abuse. I can honestly say there are years of my life I can't recall. It's funny how our mind works as a defense mechanism to protect us from trauma. My innocence was stolen. My ability to think as a normal child was gone. No child should ever have to experience this nightmare. I lived in fear, shame, and guilt. I felt cheap and dirty, like something was wrong with me. I wanted to cry out and tell somebody, but I didn't want to hurt others by exposing this secret. The older I got, I realized just how wrong this was, but I knew exposing this secret would create incredible pain and turmoil for the ones I loved. I just couldn't speak up. What if I told them and they didn't believe me or blamed me? I would lose everything that meant anything to me. I realize now that it wouldn't have happened, but when you are a child trying to reason through an adult situation, you just don't see things very clearly.

Was a normal life too much to ask for? I wanted to feel true love and security, not love polluted by perversion. So, to say the least,

I became a very good actor. No one knew or sensed my pain. As far as everyone else knew, my life on the outside was perfect, while inside I screamed out a muffled, yet desperate unheard cry for help. I did the best I could. It was hard. I blamed God and others. Inside, I resented so many for what I was going through. I felt alone; I dreaded life. I couldn't wait for the day I could take care of myself and take control of my own life.

I knew one thing for sure: I wouldn't cause myself any more pain, or so I thought. The reality is, the pain and scars left behind from sexual abuse are real. It is a taboo subject no one wants to deal with, but it is a reality for more people than we know. The scars don't show on the outside, but deep behind the curtains of our heart, they showcase themselves. They are buried deep inside, but on a constant fight for the surface; it's a constant battle to keep them buried down. It also requires a lot of energy which can lead to depression—all in an effort to stay safe. If they show up on the surface they must be dealt with, and to the hurting heart, dealing with them isn't an attractive option. For any wound to heal properly, it must have the proper attention. Sometimes the pain is too great and too scary to bear, so we keep the issues buried and out of sight. Many of us fear that the pain will crush us, so we keep it hidden or numbed. A scar should not be a reminder of the wound itself, but it should, as a pen so beautifully marks the pages of a heroic tale, tell a story of God's grace, marking the spot as a memorial of His healing. We are often too ashamed to show our scars, but they are not something to hide. Your scars are a trophy of God's infinite grace and love.

As mentioned, I had the privilege to grow up on a church pew and be raised in the church. This was such a great privilege I thank God for, but while dealing with the sexual abuse, it was very confusing for me. I remember when I was a little girl around the age of ten or so, I was so tired of suffering abuse that I ran to the altar to beg God, "Please, make this stop." Sexual abuse can be more traumatic than physical abuse. With physical abuse, everyone can see the results and many want to help, but with sexual abuse, it's less evident and help always seems elusive. The mental and emotional pain is enough to break anyone.

Situations that I had been subjected to played over and over in my mind like a film reel. I just wanted to get away. I just didn't understand why God would allow this to happen to me. I grew up singing hymns in the church such as "Yes, Jesus Loves Me" and "Jesus Loves the Little Children." So why was this happening to me? Did I do something to God? Was something wrong with me? It was impossible to understand and rationalize all of this at the age of ten. I had to carry a weight no child was meant to carry. Instead of the other kids simply praying for a new toy, I tried and sought after God for understanding. I did everything I knew to do to make sure I was protected, but it was never enough.

Because of the actions of others, I experienced pain. I had to grow up real fast. I would love to say, at that time, I didn't have feelings of resentment, bitterness, and hatred inside of me, but I did. I felt cheated, abandoned, and cheapened. When I was around others who displayed normal relationships and carefree lives, I couldn't help but be envious. It was a natural reaction to an unnatural experience.

Every person out there wants to feel loved, accepted, and secure. This is the way God made us. I was blessed beyond measure to be surrounded by an incredible youth group and leaders who loved the Lord and truly cared about me. Their guidance and influence forever impacted my life. An evangelist came through our church and prophesied over my life, telling me God had a work for me to do, that I needed to pursue it. But the truth is, I didn't know how or what I was pursuing.

Thoughts continually flooded my mind like scenes on a movie screen as I lay there on the bed of that motel room trying to make sense of this mess I was in. I began to think back to how Jim and I met. I was about six years old when a new family started coming to our church. They had a son named Jim, who was so bright and handsome. The childhood crush had officially begun. My eyes always lit up around him, and a huge smile crept over my face every time I saw him. I just knew I was "in love." It was an innocent yet heart-melting experience. Within a few months of attending our church, Jim and I forged an instant connection, as he and my brother were about the same age and soon became friends. As the years progressed, this innocent crush turned into my first kiss, and the older I got, the more intense my feelings grew. He seemed to be in and out of trouble and made some bad choices that derailed his life, but my attraction for him was so great that I was blinded to the warning signs. Soon he would move away and make a choice to not live for God.

In December 1990, the Christmas of my senior year, Jim resurfaced, as he had moved away and had come home to visit. He was now getting ready to deploy for Iraq to serve in Desert Storm. He was twenty-one; I was sixteen. I always had a secret thing for him, but due to our age differences, he was always out of my reach . . . or at least so I thought. On Christmas morning shortly after breakfast, I was watching a special on TV of different soldiers serving in Desert Storm saying hello to their families back home. I began to think of him and thought, *We've been friends for years, and I am going to call to let him know how much I care.* So I did. It was a short but sweet conversation that only intensified my feelings for him. I thought I would write him a letter to where he was stationed at Fort Hood and see what happened.

I knew my parents wouldn't approve, first of all because of the age difference but also because he had been married before and had been in trouble with the law. What they didn't know was I was going to change him. He would be different. Then, as all of these thoughts were rushing through my mind, the reality of what I had done began to set in. Even though I took this step, I was still dating the same guy I had been with since my freshman year of high school. *Oh well,* I thought, *he is just going to read my letter and laugh at me the next time we see each other.* A few days went by, and

I got busy and forgot about the letter. Then, all of a sudden, I got a letter in the mail. It was from him. He wrote that he felt the same way and would be in town the next weekend, and we could talk. I was in a real pickle now.

The weekend came and we talked, and I knew that I wasn't a good liar. I had to make a decision: break up with the guy I had dated since high school and pursue Jim, or not pursue Jim and still break up with my boyfriend. My feelings for my high school sweetheart had dwindled, and my heart wasn't into our relationship any longer. After literally making myself sick over this, I decided to pursue Jim and see what happened. I still to this day cannot tell you how I convinced my parents we were just friends and to let us spend time together, but I did. Our relationship started out great. I would go with his parents down to Fort Hood and spend the weekends with him, or he would come home and we would spend time together. To a teenage girl, it was perfect. Our relationship escalated quickly and, before my parents knew it, he had given me an engagement ring before he left to go serve with the Army during Desert Storm.

The day he left for Saudi Arabia was one of the saddest days of my life. I remember watching the soldiers board the airport bus and seeing families emotionally torn apart because of the commitment their loved one made to serve our wonderful country. It definitely gave me a healthy respect not only for our soldiers but also for the families left behind. The next few months were difficult as I found myself waiting for the mailman every day to see that one letter saying he was okay.

It was also exciting for me because I was closing one chapter of my life and celebrating my high school graduation. At the ceremony, the principal of the academy presented me with a scholarship to Baylor University. I was so surprised and excited. But it was here that I stood at a major crossroads in my life, asking myself: *Do I move forward and get my education, leaving familiar things behind; or, do I stay here, get married, and see where life takes me?*

It was pressing.

The decision of not pursuing my education will be one that I will always regret. After discussing everything with Jim, I made the decision not to go. I didn't want to leave him, but honestly, deep down, I didn't have the self-confidence to go alone. Most of all, I was scared of the unknown, but what does fear of the unknown really mean? The unknown does not exist. Our fear is based on something that literally is not there. Think of a child at a young age: they have no problem going to sleep in their room at night. Then, as they begin to grow older and see things on TV or hear stories from friends, fear suddenly starts creeping in. They begin to say, "Leave the light on, Mommy." Fear shows up at an early age. The sad part of this is, most of what we fear does not exist. Nonetheless, I didn't want to experience any more pain, fear, or loneliness; I just wanted to be rescued and live happily ever after.

After about six months, Jim came home. This was a night I will never forget. The excitement that filled the gymnasium at Fort Hood was electrifying. It was so moving to see children run to meet their moms and dads, husbands and wives unite, and parents hug their children, thanking God for their safe return.

While Jim was in Iraq, I had been hired at the Commercial National Bank as a receptionist. I enjoyed my job, but I enjoyed the money I made even more. After he got home, the battle between Jim and my parents intensified. My mother despised the very sight of him. She was not shy about voicing her opinion either, which put a huge wedge between us. I was being made to choose, and I chose him.

At that moment, I realized my choice to leave home and pursue a relationship with Jim was really an effort to find true love and security. I just wanted to get away from the pain of one area of my life, and so I jumped ship into an unknown place. But to me, the unknown served as tangible hope for escape from the empty, broken, and painful world that I did know. I thought this would be the best way. The Devil is masterful at making the wrong choices look right.

But if we would turn to God instead of away from Him, listening to His still, small voice deep in our souls, it would prevent us from living as slaves to perpetual bad choices, running from our past.

The haze of the overdose was wearing off. As I lay there taking in the surroundings of that motel room, I watched as Jim kept using drugs. His lack of concern for what had just happened crushed me. *What had I done to my life?* I thought. I felt hopeless. I began to cry out to God, asking *"WHY?"* I wanted to run, but all I had to go back to was bad memories, and I knew without a shadow of doubt, I didn't want that. I cried until it felt as though my eyes dried up and withered, and I drifted off to sleep.

The next thing I knew, the phone began to ring in the motel room, and the sun pierced through a crack in the curtains. It was morning. I began to feel for the phone and said hello. It was the motel office calling, saying I had a guest who would like to see me. I asked who and they said, "Your dad." I was shocked. What was *he* doing here? How did he track me down? Frankly, I was scared out of my senses. As I got up to get ready, I felt as though a truck hit me. I was so weak and tired; I just simply didn't feel well. As I brushed my teeth and hair and threw on some clothes, my mind began to race as to why he was here. Jim was reluctant to let me go. He was afraid my dad wouldn't let me come back. I didn't know. I have to admit there was a part of me screaming for him to help me and another part of me rebelling, "Leave me alone. I'm doing okay, but please save me." I never dreamed the first time I used drugs that I would need saving. For me, the first time I used was out of curiosity, but it soon became a way of escape. Once again, I found myself putting on a mask to cover the pain and act like I had it all together.

As I walked down the stairs, legs wobbling and twitching, I could see my dad standing by his truck. He looked rough, as though he had been up all night. When I got downstairs, he wrapped his arms around me and began to cry. At that moment, I had a hundred emotions flooding my heart. I didn't know what to do with them all. He asked me if he could take me to breakfast, to which I agreed. He drove me to the nearest Denny's, and we sat and talked. As he talked, he began to sob, creating a scene. It felt as though everyone at the restaurant was staring a hole right through us.

He said in a fit of tears, "I had to come find you. Are you okay?"

I said, "Yes, why? Dad, please be quiet, everyone is staring at us."

He quickly asked his next question, giving little regard to my request, "Did anything happen to you last night?"

I said, "No, why?"

"Well, your granny came by the house last night after church and said, 'We have to find Misty. I am scared something is terribly wrong with her, and I fear for her life.'"

My parents began to ask why, and she told them what had just happened a few hours ago during their church service. She said that it was a normal Wednesday night service. It was very predictable. They sang a few choruses and Brother Jones got up to read a chapter from the book of Proverbs. But this time, it was different. He began to read as normal, but shortly after he began, he stopped and said, "Church, I feel strongly impressed of God to stop and ask for every saint to begin to cry out for mercy for one of our own children who has strayed. If we do not intercede on their behalf, they will die."

My grandmother said she immediately felt by the impression of God that it was me. She said that a deep prayer began to fill the sanctuary, and instead of having a predictable Wednesday night service, they had a prayer meeting. Just like seventeen years prior when I was a baby, God reached down, answered a prayer for me, and with the mercy only He can show, spared my life.

As he told me this, I could feel goose bumps and the hair rising stiffly on my arms. I knew God knew right where I was and, in His mercy, had His saints intercede for me when I was in no shape to pray for myself. I could not hold back the tears. They fell like water from a faucet. I never told my dad what happened, but he knew it was for me. My pride would not allow me to come clean. The Bible says that pride cometh before a fall. I was destined to fall again.

As I returned to the motel room, I really didn't know what to expect. I wasn't sure if Jim would be there or if he would be angry because I left. To my surprise, he was just happy I came back.

3

IN TOO DEEP

One would think after a close call with death, and experiencing God's grace and mercy, a person would change their ways. Well, I didn't. I found myself using again, with a total disregard for what God had done. I was a professional at playing games and hiding behind a mask. I would go to church and try to live a life free of the chains that held me bound, but I still had not yet learned the secret of living in relationship with God. Trying to live this life on my own, I found myself struggling with my addictions again. Before I knew it, I relapsed and began using again. To prove I was in control and could handle life, I refused to turn to God, but instead began using drugs more heavily than before.

I ran from the pain of my past and fear of what my future held. Truth is, when I was around fifteen, I felt a call of God upon my life but had no direction or understanding of what that call meant or how to surrender to it. All I knew was what I felt in my spirit and that it was something different. I just assumed I was a broken girl that God could never use. I convinced myself that I had missed call altogether, and the prophecies that I had received during youth just meant I needed to be a good saint. I allowed con- demnation and shame from the abuse to keep me from God rather than draw me to Him and seek His direction. I was ashamed. It was like I was on a mission of self-destruction, and I was very good at it. I hated life, and I felt as though I had nothing to live for. It seemed that every time I would try and turn my life back over to God, it was just for a short period of time, and then I would relapse.

I fell harder into my drug addiction, finding myself entangled deeper than ever before. I tried to get well within my own power, and realizing I couldn't, I gave up. I was on a mission, chasing the rush of my first high. Oh, how sin can enslave you so quickly. I found myself pawning everything I owned, stealing, and using any and everyone I could to get money for my next fix. I wanted so badly to be in control of my life, but the truth is, you will always be sold out to something.

Your choices are influenced by your past and your perception of your self-worth. The choice is yours: destruction in sin or freedom in God. A choice is easily made from the perimeter, but it's all too difficult to make when you're trying to coach and play the game at the same time. Scripture tells us, "Straight is the gate, and narrow is the way, which leadeth unto life, and few there be that find it" (Matt. 7:14). There are many who travel this path. The narrow road looks hard and full of rules and restrictions, while the wide road looks pleasing to the natural eye and full of pleasure. The ironic thing is, looks are deceiving: the narrow road provides freedom and the wide road enslaves you.

I couldn't see this, and I kept doing anything I could to please my selfish desires. At the age of seventeen, I would frequently find myself on a drug binge for days.

I quickly found myself in a state of desperation. I needed money to afford my addiction, and a lot of it. At the recommendation of a couple of friends, I found myself inside of a strip club, asking if they were hiring for a job as a waitress. I didn't want to be a stripper, but

I heard you could get good tips by being a waitress. I learned quickly the power of seduction and planned to use it for my own gain. I knew my mom and granny would kill me; after all, they raised me to know better. But it was just another rush, another thrill to do something I knew was wrong. As I approached one of the employees and asked if they were hiring, he asked me to come back a couple of days later and meet with the owner. So I did. After meeting with him, I was immediately offered the job and was instructed to come back in and pick up my uniform on Thursday. I was to start immediately.

As God would have it, a friend of my brother's told him that he saw me at this strip club. As you can imagine, my phone began to blow up with family members asking me what in the world I was doing. My brother called and told me if he found this to be true, he would tell my granny, and God knows I didn't want to disappoint her any more. Deep down inside, I didn't want to be in that environment. With the deep fears that I had of being raped or killed, I called the owner back and told him I was not going to be able to take the job. God never let go of me.

But the desperation I felt was overwhelming. I knew I needed to stop, but I couldn't. The physical pain and craving I felt due to my addiction drove my every move. I became the opposite, the dark twin of everything I had been before. One evening, the craving for drugs blinded my better judgment. I called the dealer and met him at his house at about one in the morning, begging for an eight ball of cocaine, telling him that I would pay him back later when I got the money. He told me if I performed sexual acts for him, he would not make me pay him back. In a second, I came face-to-face with my fear. All I could think about was running. No longer was I thinking about the drug itself.

Sitting in the truck, engine purring, I whispered the name of Jesus in my head, praying He would listen and come to my rescue. When I told the dealer no, I saw the anger fill his eyes as he sat in the passenger seat. Fear rushed in. Right then, the truck made a loud popping noise like a gunshot, and the two men in my truck got scared and left. God had protected me once again. Then the dealer threw the cocaine at me and told me I better get him the money within a couple of days or he would come find me. I knew I didn't have the money, so I called my mom and told her what I had done. She gave me the money to go pay the dealer so he wouldn't come after me. I am alive today only because of the grace and mercy of God.

I disappointed so many people and ruined my reputation, but when you are in the middle of your pain, that's the last thing you think of. I went from being looked up to and respected to a drug addict, one that everyone tried to help but quickly gave up on when they realized they couldn't help someone who didn't want to help herself. This was one choice I would have to make for myself. My own choices got me into this mess, and it would be my own choices that got me out.

As harsh as it may sound, I felt like a human pincushion as I shot up. A big thanks to God I didn't have good veins. Once I shot up and missed so many times, I lacerated my skin, which led to an infection in my right arm. At the poor advice of those around me, I took a razor blade and began to cut my arm to allow the infection to drain. I can still hear the screams of intense pain I made as I dug the razor blade into my arm. I knew I had no choice but to go home to my mom, show her what I had done, and ask for help. My bony right arm had swelled to twice its size by the time I got to her.

She immediately rushed me to the nearest emergency room. Of course, every nurse and doctor seemed to enjoy watching me suffer, at least that's how I remember it. I thought they were trying to teach me a lesson. After several hours in the emergency room and many tests, they admitted me in the hospital and started IV antibiotics. A sigh of relief swept over me, and I felt safe and loved every moment my mom sat beside me.

Shortly after I got to my room, I became deathly ill, throwing up about every five minutes. I looked at my mom and told her to call my family. At that moment, I felt as if I was going to die. Doctors and nurses ran in and out of my room. They brought in an X-ray machine to do some sort of test, believing this was an allergic reaction to the penicillin, but wanting to rule out anything else. They immediately gave me drugs to counteract the antibiotic. After a couple of hours of receiving the medication, I was able to rest. By the next morning, my arm was now swollen to at least three times its normal size. It looked like it would explode at any moment. When the doctor came in, he sat by my bedside as I held my mother's hand. He informed us I needed emergency surgery, and there was a high probability that if the infection had reached my bloodstream, he would have to amputate my right arm in an effort to save my life.

My mom and I broke down, tears surging down our faces. I thought about death or life without my arm, and I was overwhelmed with so many different emotions. But after discussing it with my mom, we told the doctor to do whatever it took to save my life. The doctor exited the room, saying as soon as an operating room came available, he would be in to get me. It wasn't very long until the anesthesiologist and nurses came to wheel me to the operating room. My family didn't know what to expect. They didn't know if I would live or learn to manage life without an arm. My mom called all of her family and the church, asking them to pray. The doctor told my mom the surgery would take about an hour, but as the hour mark ticked by, my mom was informed it was more serious than they had thought. They assured her I was okay but that the surgery would take longer than expected. After two hours of surgery, the doctor came out to let my family know I was okay. He saved my arm but said he was glad he went in when he did. If he had waited another day, the infection would have hit my bloodstream. The infection was but a hairline away from my veins. I had a long way to go with regard to recovery, he said. But he only hoped and prayed, along with my family, that this experience would have an everlasting impact.

My family began to thank God for His mercy and rejoice that, once again, God had spared my life. The next thing I knew, as I was regaining consciousness and being wheeled to my room, there were at least thirty to forty family members and friends standing outside my room—some I hadn't seen for years. They were thanking God for His miracle-working power. I felt so blessed even though the recovery was very painful. Regaining the use of my arm seemed like a never-ending process. During my recovery, I had plenty of time to evaluate my life and contemplate where things went wrong.

All of my elementary years through the seventh grade, I went to a local Christian school. The environment was good and the influences were positive. The summer between my seventh and eighth grade year, I decided I wanted to go to a public school. After convincing my parents, the new adventure began. A different world opened up to me, and I realized just how sheltered I was. I saw fights in the lunchroom, guys smoking, and couples kissing in the hallways. To say the least, I was in culture shock. This kind of behavior would have gotten you kicked out of school in a New York minute where I came from. Over a short period of time, the shock factor wore off and soon everything began to seem normal. Looking back, man was I sheltered.

At the end of my eighth grade year, I searched to find a crowd I could fit into, and it was not easy. I remember going to a meeting to be on the high school pep squad, and I made the team. I was so excited. As I started high school, I was all about having fun and being popular, even though most of the things I involved myself in stood in direct opposition to everything that I knew was right. I quickly found my way into the popular crowd and began dating one of the most popular guys in the school. I was voted class president and went from being in the pep squad to the drill team the very next year. I was having a great time. My social life was going well, and high school was so much fun. I had always been a straight-A student, with an occasional B. Let's just say my grades began to drop as my focus quickly changed from books to boys. I began to skip school and be promiscuous. Still, in my own mind, I wasn't a bad girl.

As I looked around me, I saw others smoking, drinking, and doing drugs. I would say to myself, "At least I'm not doing that." It was midway through my sophomore year when God really began to deal with my behavior. I was still going to church every Sunday and Wednesday, and I faithfully attended every youth event. Nobody at my church worried about me. It appeared as though I was doing fine. I had become a pro at making things look one way, when in reality they were quite the contrary. One Sunday evening, an evangelist named Shannon Stanley came to visit my church, Calvary Tabernacle. He preached straight to me. God quickly began to deal with my heart. While I was at the altar praying, my mind reminisced of how close I once was to God and how quickly it seemed that I had become distant and cold. I remembered fasting and praying and how good it felt to feel God wrap His arms around me. I remember coming to the altar when the call for response was given, pouring my heart out to God in repentance, and pledging to begin anew.

Monday morning came very early, as I had to be at school at 6:30 a.m. every morning for drill team practice. I remember getting there and sitting in my car, listening to music and praying or just reading my Bible. I felt trapped. In reality, I probably wasn't, but let's all face it: perception can be as powerful as reality. It's all in what you believe in. God began to convict my heart and draw me closer to Him. I finished that year out on drill team, and I began to convince my mom and dad I needed to go to my church's school the following year. It was very easy to do since, during my sophomore year, there was a shooting in the entrance of my high school next to the principal's office, just before the tardy bell rang. It was gang related. My parents were concerned for my safety and allowed me to transfer. I was very excited. I felt that this move would be a safe haven for me, not only physically but also spiritually as well. I worked very hard during the next year of school, completing my junior and senior year in one year. Now, I felt grown. I was going to take control of my life. In reality, this is where it all started going wrong: when I took my life out of God's hands and into my own. I chose to pursue a relationship despite everyone's best warnings, but I thought I knew better. So I didn't listen.

I began to see glimpses of what my parents were warning me about, but how could I ever admit this to them? I was determined to change things so that I could prove my parents wrong. Oh, how I wish I had paid heed to the warning signs. One afternoon, as I was at work at the bank shortly after Jim arrived home from Desert Storm, I got a call from Jim wanting to know when I was coming over. I could tell he had been drinking; his words were slurred. Up to this point, I had never seen him drunk. I saw him drink a beer or two, but that was about it. When I arrived at his parents' home where he was staying, he was riding his dirt bike in the street and was so drunk he could barely steer, let alone hold the bike. To be blunt, I was scared. I may have been subjected to sexual abuse, which in itself is horrendous, but to see someone completely out of their own control scared me to death.

He was belligerent. He was looking for a fight. I began to talk to him, only to be slammed up against a wall and told to shut up. I burst into tears, scared to say another word. I immediately left in fear, but before going home I knew I had to compose myself; my family would kill him if they knew what had happened. As I sat at home that evening, I began to justify that the only reason he did that was because he was drunk, and if we could talk when he was sober, this would never happen again. We all know there is no reasoning with a drunken individual. You would have more success conversing with a toddler.

Later that night, as he began to sober up, he called me to apologize and asked me what I was doing with him. He began to tell me how he didn't deserve someone as good as me and would understand if I left. I couldn't hold back the tears and began to tell him it was okay, that we would work past this. Before I could hang up the phone we exchanged "I love yous," and I felt as though life was re-solved and everything would go back to the way it had been before.

Unfortunately, this event became the norm. Once again, I found myself victimized—this time, by physical abuse. It started out with a push, excused because of alcohol. Then it was a slap, but this time he was sober. I had disagreed with him on how he was acting and conducting his life. He didn't like my interference, and the slap made that abundantly clear.

Why do I stay? I kept asking myself. Yet I repeatedly pushed the questions away into silence. A few weeks passed and he obtained employment. It was the norm for me to come over when I got off work, but this day was different. From about noon on, I was unable to get him on the phone. When I got home from work, I called his parents' house to see if he had made it home yet because I just knew something had happened to his phone. His mom said she had not seen or heard from him. She thought he was with me. I thought to myself, *No, this is too weird.*

Several hours later, at approximately 10:00 p.m., I tried his mom's number again, only to hear her say he wasn't there. I could tell she was just as worried as I was, but she made excuses in the hope of making me feel better. To say the least, I didn't sleep all night. I began to call every local hospital, and the local jails too, just to see if something had happened. He had been in trouble with the law before, but I overlooked those details, refusing to see the bad and only looking at the good.

The next morning, I went to work, sleep-deprived, eyes swol-len from crying all night, suffering through a helpless feeling of what I had done to make him do this to me. As soon as the company he worked for opened up, I called them to see if he was there, and they told me no. Apparently, he and one other guy abandoned their work truck at an apartment complex, and they had not heard from them since. Now I was really worried. What if they had been robbed and were left somewhere for dead? I was a basket case, but I somehow managed to hold it together and stay at work.

Later on that afternoon, as I answered the phone at work, I heard his voice on the other end of the line. He said he was sorry and needed me to come to this motel so he could talk to me. He gave me directions and, despite the knot of fear I had in my stomach, I went. No one knew where I was going; I just left. As I pulled into the parking lot of the motel, I saw several rough characters and became nervous for my own safety. I made it up the stairs to the motel room door and knocked; he opened the door.

As I walked in, he walked over and sat me on the bed. I lashed out one question after another, as now I was confident he was cheating on me and braced myself for the one sentence, "I need to tell you something." The words he said next were unbelievable, and I knew I was in trouble. He told me he was addicted to cocaine and needed help to overcome the addiction.

At that moment, I looked down at the table and saw syringes. In the trashcan next to it were more of them. I have never been so scared in my life. I felt as though I was in over my head. How could I help someone overcome drug addiction? I had drunk a couple of wine coolers before, but other than that, I didn't know the first thing about drugs. I was just adjusting to the fact he had abused alcohol, and now he was telling me about his addiction to cocaine. I should have run that day, but instead of leaving or getting him help, I let my guard down and over time found myself a slave to drugs as well.

As I sat there evaluating my life, I began to think how foolish I was. I clearly saw the mistakes I had made to this point but found myself in over my head and didn't know how to get out.

While I was recovering from my surgery, Jim and I began going to church again. We did all we knew to do to be right. Throughout our relationship, Jim was constantly in and out of jail for parole violations due to drugs. It was during one of the times he ran from the police that he decided to really give God his all. He opened up and began to talk to me about the call of God he felt upon his life to preach. We really tried living for God and did great for a short period of time, but we allowed fears of the future and things of life to creep up and separate us from our daily relationship with the Lord.

Then, before we knew it, the addictions we had been delivered from once again began to infiltrate our lives. We were captive to the chains of drugs, alcohol, and immorality. It seemed every time we went back, the chains became stronger. How would we ever be set free? My family began to think, *Is this going to be her life until it kills her?* My mom said NO, and after being away from the Lord for over ten years, she found herself flat on her face praying for me day after day. God dealt with my family, bringing them back to Him one by one. It seemed as though my situation was being used for His glory.

My mom struggled with feelings of hatred, as any mother would. She hated the sight of Jim and wished he would leave. He was in and out of jail, and it seemed as though when he was in jail, her daughter would give her life to God, but as soon as he would get out, something would happen and her little girl would fall back into the dark and violent storm of drugs. Despite her prayers, it seemed my drug addiction worsened. No matter how hopeless my mom felt, she knew God was the only answer. He had the power to deliver her daughter from the chains that enslaved her. My family was so desperate to rescue me that they obtained a court order for my arrest to have me brought in for a psychiatric evaluation. They hoped the doctors would be able to determine I was addicted and a danger to myself, and that I would be admitted for treatment. They thought anyone that could do the things that I had done must have some psychiatric issues.

One New Year's Eve afternoon, after I fell back into my addiction at the young age of seventeen, I went to my cousin Starla's house for a shower after being on a drug binge for days. I had plans to quickly leave and meet some people, partying the old year out and the New Year in. My cousin Starla was my rock, my best friend. She was always there for me, in the good times and the bad. She loved me as her own child and was distraught over the poor choices I had made in my life. I felt safe for the brief moment I was there, but as

I walked out of the bathroom, I saw two men standing in the living room stating we need to talk. As any rebellious teenager would do at this point in their life, I lashed out with words of anger, demanding a reason. They said my family had gotten a court order for me to be taken in for evaluation.

I can't describe the hate I felt. My mind raced as I tried to scheme a plan to get away. They reached out to grab my arms, and I told them I just got out of the shower and needed to get dressed. My plan was to jump out the window as soon as I shut the door, but it was evident they knew my plan. I was humiliated as these two men turned their backs in the room with me as I got my clothes on. I knew there was no escaping this. They had me. Anger boiled inside me as I hurriedly dressed myself. My own family did this to me. They knew I was not crazy. I knew in my mind they wanted to help me, but I couldn't help but fill myself with rage with how they handled this. Why would they do this to me?

After I got dressed, they asked me to turn around so that they could handcuff me. I began to plead with them, "Please, please do not handcuff me." I said. "I am 105 pounds soaking wet. Please do not do this." One of the two men was extremely sweet, and he and I made a connection that I can't explain. He rode in the backseat with me as the other man drove me in for evaluation. I remember trying to act tough on the outside, but inside, I was a little child screaming for help, and all I wanted was my momma. I couldn't stop the river of tears flowing down my cheeks. The gentleman sitting by me looked at me and said, "Girl, what are you doing? Why are you doing this to yourself? Your family loves you so much and wants to help you."

I began to tell him I didn't have a problem and that I was fine. My parents were just trying to "control" me. None of that was true, but it was how I felt at the time. They just wanted me back, drug free and healthy. I will always remember his uplifting words, telling me I was too good to be doing this and that I deserved a better life for myself. For the life of me, I can't remember his name, but he for-

ever impacted me because of his genuine concern for m[y]
ing. The drive to the hospital seemed way too quick. As we p[ ]
up to the back entrance, I truly felt like I was living a scene from a
movie. After the car pulled to a stop and I got out, I clung to the one
officer's arm, for I was truly scared to death.

As we approached the door, out came the largest man I had ever
seen, wearing a white nurse's uniform. By this time I broke down.
The tough guy act went out the window. I looked at the gentlemen
whose arm I would not let go of and cried, "Please, please don't
leave me here. I am scared. I am not crazy, I just made stupid choices."

He looked at me with big tears in his eyes. He told his partner to
go to the car and wait for him. He was not leaving me until he knew
I was going to be okay. He stayed with me for a while, but it only
felt like a few seconds. He didn't leave until I was safe in a room.
He told me what to expect, that he had spoken with nurses he personally knew and they assured him they would take care of me. I
remember sitting in that room waiting for a psychiatrist to come
and evaluate me, asking myself, *What are you doing here, Misty?*

My life had spun out of control fast, but I wasn't ready to give in
and do the right thing. I kept fighting. I saw a phone in the room
and called Jim to let him know where I was. He assured me he was
on his way and instructed me what to say and how to act, as he had
been through this before. Within a few minutes, the psychiatrist
walked in to evaluate me. She asked me a series of questions. After
I answered, she left, and a nurse came in to let me know my family
was there to see me. As any hateful, rebellious person would do, I
refused to see them. The nurse came back in and said, "They are
begging to see you."

For some reason, I said I would only see my mom and my
brother. I have to admit that when they walked in the room and my
mom's arms wrapped around my neck, it was just what I needed at
that moment. But I sure didn't let them know that. I visited with
them for a few minutes, and within an hour or two, the psychia-

trist came in and said they were releasing me, as they did not have grounds to hold me. I got a lengthy lecture, but that was all. I would like to say that this traumatic experience changed me, but instead it made me bitter and more determined to show them all I didn't need them. I could handle my own life.

Not very long after this, Jim was arrested and went back to jail. Every time he was sent back to jail, the sentence became longer and longer. I managed to get ahold of myself and, with Jim's encouragement, get back into the church. I think he was just scared I would find someone else. It was not long after this we married. I was finally eighteen, and no one could stop me. I knew better than to get married to him, but I had such low self-esteem that I didn't think anyone else would want me nor did I deserve better. I poured my heart and soul into our relationship, and although I was far from perfect, I tried to make it work with everything in me.

4

IT'S TIME TO CHANGE

Misery. Pain. Darkness. The cycle of addiction controlled my life. My body became skeleton-like, and I began to grow weary of the life that I was living. Ironically, God had begun to work in my life, but I couldn't even see it. I was tired of being in a relationship where I felt as though I was the only one giving. I was tired of living with a man I couldn't trust, the constant fear of him cheating on me, saying the wrong thing, and being subject to more physical abuse or the never-ending emotional abuse that always made me feel less than the woman deep down I knew that I was. I tried to leave many times, but every time I would give in and go back, afraid that one day he would live out the threats of suicide he often made whenever I threatened to leave him. I felt trapped, like a silent mouse in a maze.

I grew weary of living and knew that if something didn't change, I would end up dead. If not by overdose, Jim would accidentally kill me in a moment of rage. The man I fell in love with was no longer there. Gone. Deep down inside he was just as troubled as

I was, running from God, refusing to surrender to God's plan for his life. Drugs had taken over both of us, and we had become toxic for one another. We had a special way of bringing out the worst in each other.

One Saturday afternoon after we picked up an eight ball of cocaine and drove back to the apartment to use, I told him I was not going to do drugs that night. I wanted to go to church in the morning. He was shocked at my decision, but deep down inside, he knew I couldn't resist once the drugs were in front of me. As we entered the apartment, I begin to pray under my breath, "God, if you want me to go to church, you are going to have to help me."

As Jim began to use, I lay on the floor, literally shaking, fighting the urge to vomit as my body began to crave the cocaine. As tears began to flow down my face, I begged God to let me go to sleep, fearing I would give in to temptation if I did not fall asleep soon; I didn't trust myself. The next thing I knew, the sun was piercing through the blinds as if to say good morning. I woke up with an intense feeling of gratitude that God allowed me to go to sleep and not use. I looked around, and there he was—my husband, still using. An intense sadness I cannot describe dropped into my heart when I saw the waste of what our lives had become.

Sobbing uncontrollably as I was getting ready for church, I could not wait to get to the house of God. I felt such an intense pull to get there. As I walked through the doors of New Life Tabernacle, I found myself a seat at the back of the church. They worshipped and sang songs of praise that brought peace to my troubled soul. I felt an intense desire to worship, but the heaviness of condemnation kept me from raising my arms. I began to feel out of place like, "What am I doing here?" In my humanity, I wanted to run, but the Spirit within me beckoned me to stay. As always, Pastor B. E. Stanley preached passionately, led of the Spirit of God with every word. As he began to conclude his message, I wanted to run to the front for prayer, but I felt like a shell of a person, empty. I truly didn't have the strength to make it there. I fought my own pride because

I knew that if I went to the altar to pray, it would scream, "Look, I made a mess of my life. I need help." That was just too vulnerable for me; after all, I was strong. I was in control. I had all of this together, right?

I truly don't know if anyone knew how bad my drug abuse had gotten, but I knew one thing to be true: if I kept using, I was going to die. God had a plan and was not letting me go that day without touching my life. There was a lady by the name of Linda who let God use her in a miraculous way that day. She walked up to me and began to talk and pray with me, and it was like the dam of my emotions broke. I began to sob uncontrollably, asking God for forgiveness and to help me change. I prayed and cried out to God with everything within me. Then the power of God fell on me. I began to speak with other tongues as the Spirit of God gave me the ability. God had re-filled me once again with the baptism of His Spirit. I can't describe to you the joy I felt inside. That moment, God replaced the immense heaviness within me with peace. I was elated, light and lifted up. I didn't want to leave the church, not wanting to ever lose the presence and power of God that I was feeling at that very moment. The people of God surrounded me, and I remember the affection that Sister Glenda Stanley showed me that day. Her hug was that of a mother, my spiritual mother. She cried and prayed with me. I felt so secure in her arms. It was as if she was going to battle for me in the Spirit as she prayed. Brother and Sister Stanley encouraged me, and I will never forget the genuine love of God they both showed me.

As church ended and it was time to go home, I knew what I had to face. God helped me. I cannot describe the strength God gave me that day. The courage and willpower I showed was without a doubt not of my own power; it was God. He was orchestrating my steps, little did I know.

"The LORD shall fight for you, and ye shall hold your peace" (Exod. 14:14).

After I got back to the apartment, my husband asked me how

the service had gone. I told him how I felt and how sick I was of this life that we were leading together. To my surprise, he broke, and we both prayed. He even agreed to go to church with me, but he wanted to go to a different church. I was so elated that he wanted to go to church and pursue a drug-free life that I followed him to whichever church he chose. I knew God was everywhere, and as long as God was with me, I could survive.

It was as if God opened the windows of heaven and began to bless us. We went to church that evening, and God re-filled Jim with the gift of the Holy Ghost as well. It was like we went from a life of sin, darkness, and pain to living in complete victory. God had begun a work in us. We attended church every time the doors opened and even weeknight prayer meetings. God truly was at work.

A month or so had passed, and I found myself extremely tired, eating like never before. Feelings of nausea consumed my days at different times. I thought I was fighting off the flu, but Jim told me that he thought I was pregnant. I said, "Oh no, surely not." I have to say, the idea of pregnancy crossed my mind, but the very thought of it scared me to death, so I denied it and went on like nothing was wrong. One Friday evening as we ate dinner with a few couples from church, the subject was brought up about the possibility of me being pregnant. Two of the women there said, "Well, let's find out."

They were convinced I was pregnant, so they drove me to the store to buy a pregnancy test. When we got back to their home, I took the test. The positive reading was instant; I was pregnant. When the reality of this hit me, I sat down and began to cry out of fear. I was barely able to take care of myself, much less a baby. Then the thought hit me, how could I tell my mom? She couldn't stand Jim for what he had done to me, but little did I know, God had already been at work on Momma too.

She told me that right before I made the decision to go to church, she had been praying for me, as she had done every day after she got off work. God spoke to her and told her that I needed something that I loved more than Jim to get me out of this destructive lifestyle. She then humbled herself and prayed that I would have Jim's child. This was definitely not my mom's first choice. If you asked my mom, she'd tell you: this was the hardest prayer she had ever prayed. But the reality was, even if it tied me to Jim, this child would tie me to God as well.

Jim agreed to go with me to tell my mom. I called and told her I was going to stop by on Saturday if she was home, and she quickly said, "Come on." Shortly after arriving, I told her I thought I was pregnant. But I didn't tell her I already knew. I could see the fear in her eyes as she drove us to the store to get a pregnancy test. Of course, when we arrived back home and took the test, a positive sign appeared. To my surprise, my mom didn't cry. She showed a silent strength that I didn't understand, but was deeply thankful for. I was so glad I had the support of my mom. She was then and is to this day one of my best friends. She has stuck with me through thick and thin. I didn't really know what to do next, but my mom helped me figure it out, one step at a time. I never even thought much about the fact that I didn't have insurance, but it became very evident that I needed it. My mother found a clinic at St. Paul Medical Center in Dallas that helped me get approved for Medicaid, and they took excellent care of me all the way through.

The pregnancy advanced well and seemed to be progressing normally. At approximately sixteen weeks, the clinic informed me that it was time for a blood test that would help detect any problems with the baby such as Down syndrome, so I took the test. I will never forget the day I got a call from the clinic and the nurse asked me to come back to the office. My blood work showed that my baby had a very high probability of having Down syndrome. She urged me to return to the clinic in the next couple of days, saying they would do a sonogram to determine the age of the baby and rerun the test if possible. As I sat in the room where they check your vitals, the nurse got called away to take care of something and left my chart there. I read where the doctor suggested I get counseling on what Down syndrome was and the effects it had on the baby.

I shook to the very core of my being as I tried to come to grips with what I had just read. When the nurse came back in to take my vitals, I tried to hide the fact that I was upset, but my blood pressure told the story. It was off-the-charts high. She asked me if I was all right, because my blood pressure was always normal. When she asked the question, I broke and confessed I read my chart and didn't know what to do. She immediately took me back into a room, laid me down, and began talking with me about my options. They told me this test was not 100 percent accurate and the only way I could know for sure was for them to do an amniocentesis. The risk of a miscarriage was high. They asked me what I would do if I found out my baby had Down syndrome, and I said nothing. An abortion was not an option. Then they said there was no reason to do the amniocentesis, because the risk of losing the baby was far too great. They went ahead and did the sonogram as scheduled, and that day I realized God had blessed me with a baby boy. I left there unsure of the health of my child, so I did the only thing I knew to do; turn it over to God.

The news of this was a little too much for Jim to handle. Before I knew it, he had left me and not returned home. He went back to a life filled with drugs and all of the baggage that came with it. A few days later he reappeared, apologizing for his behavior, and thus, the cycle of abuse began again. Instead of being protective of me carrying his child, he became distant and cold, as if I didn't matter. He told me he wasn't attracted to me anymore and had developed a very short fuse for anything I did. I found myself being subjected again to physical and emotional abuse; I just couldn't take it.

When I was six months pregnant, Jim and I moved to a larger apartment in preparation for the birth of our son. Our marriage was far from happy, but we managed to move forward, thinking everything was going to work out. One afternoon after he got off of work, Jim began drinking. The more he drank, the bolder his actions became. Aware of his behavior when he drank, I called my mom and told her I was going to come over and stay the night. I didn't want any trouble with Jim, and I knew if I said the wrong thing, it could result in setting him off. I didn't feel like fighting, so I told him I was going to spend time at my mother's and left.

It wasn't supposed to turn out this way, I thought. I was supposed to make something of myself. Nobody plans on making a wreck of their lives. The problem is, as youth we feel we know it all. We refuse to listen to the voices of wisdom in our lives. I felt so alone. All of my friends had moved on, and I felt as though I had no one that understood me. My family only saw things *their* way, refusing to hear any other angles. Even as low as my life had become, I still thought I could handle everything and pull myself up from this pit of despair on my own. Oh, how deceived I was.

"There is a way which seemeth right unto a man, but the end thereof are the ways of death" (Prov. 14:12).

I was not at a place where I would respond to the truth. The fact is, I knew the truth, but I didn't want to accept it. I was arrogant enough to believe I could make things okay all on my own. I could look at people and say, "SEE, I did it." But oh, how I dreaded walking into my parents' home.

They may not have said it, but I knew that coming back to their home to spend the night was giving them just the ammunition they needed to say, "I told you so." I walked into my old room and stayed mostly to myself, not in the mood to talk. Tired before I even arrived, I went to bed. I knew that as I dozed off to sleep, Jim was partying. What could I do? Nothing. Not in my condition, so off to sleep I went. In the wee hours of the night, I awoke and the Lord spoke to me and told me in a still, small voice, "Your husband is having an affair." You may think I am crazy, but I know God woke me up to prepare me for what I was to encounter next. As I contemplated what I had just heard, I shrugged it off in disbelief and went back to sleep.

The next morning, when I woke up after a good night's rest, I remembered what happened during the night. That is when I became a little concerned and said I might need to go check it out. The more I thought about him partying while I stayed at my parents' house to rest, the angrier I became, so I told my mom I was leaving to head home to see what damage had been done. She tried to encourage me otherwise, but I refused to comply with her wishes. The more I contemplated the possibility of his disloyalty, the angrier I became.

When I got to the apartment, I couldn't open the door with my key. Jim had locked the top lock; he would have to let me in. I began to bang on the door, and after a few minutes he came to the door, disheveled and still hung over from the night before. I walked in telling him I came for a change of clothes. As I went to the closet to pull out the outfit, I said to myself that I didn't even want to change in front of him. I saw all of the beer cans and trash in the living room and felt disgusted, having just organized our new apartment. As I walked out of the room to the bathroom to change, he asked me where I was going and I answered, "To change."

As I went into the bathroom, I was faced with the evidence of his infidelity: he had been unfaithful. I was angry, hurt, humiliated, and betrayed. "Why?" I screamed. "I have done everything for you. Whatever you ask I do, and whatever you want you get. Why am I not enough?"

At that point I pushed him and went to walk out the door. Before I could get to the door, I felt his hand grab me as he said, "You're not going anywhere."

I fought back to get away, but being six months pregnant made it a difficult task. The last thing I wanted was for him to touch me. It made my skin crawl. At that point he slapped me, knocking me down, and sat on me, choking me until I couldn't breathe. After a fierce struggle I managed by the grace of God to get away, and I ran to a pay phone by the pool at our apartments to call the police. Up to this point, I had never reported his abuse. I made excuses for it. But now there was a deep feeling of anger that filled me, and I just didn't care anymore. His behavior was endangering more than just me. My baby was at stake.

After speaking to the police, I called my mom, and within minutes, it seemed, she was there. The police arrived just a few minutes before my mom did and took my report before taking him to jail. As strange as it may sound, I had mixed emotions. I wanted him to pay for what he had done to me, but at the same time I wanted to fix everything and have a good life. Within a couple of hours of arriving back at my parents' home, I started having contractions. My mom took me to St. Paul Hospital to be checked out. After being evaluated by a team of doctors and nurses, they determined that I had a slight tear in my bag of water. They advised me to take it easy, that the tear was minor enough that it should heal itself, and assured me that I should be able to have a successful delivery.

After this event in my life, I moved back in with my parents. I needed to get my life together. I was left with a broken heart, broken dreams, and a sense of hopelessness. But even with all of this going on, my focus was directed toward the life that was growing inside of me. My concern was to take care of myself so that my baby would be okay. I had made a mess of my life, and the reality was I had to get it together because I was now bringing another life into the world that needed me, all of me. I began attending church, doing what I knew was right, and began to find peace. I dealt with the tremendous guilt of everything I had done and battled condemnation. I lived in fear that something would be wrong with my child. One Sunday evening at church, the Spirit of God was very strong in the sanctuary in a very powerful way, and while I was praying, a lady came up to me and gave me a word of prophesy: "God told me to tell you your baby is going to be okay." I cannot begin to tell you the emotions that flooded my soul. The gratefulness, the thanksgiving I felt was overwhelming. I could not stop crying. I was so thankful that God had heard my cry. After all, no one knew what I was going through, as I was too embarrassed to tell anyone less they judge me. God really did know just where I was, and He loved me unconditionally, even in the middle of my mess.

On an icy November morning the day after Thanksgiving, I gave birth to a healthy, beautiful baby boy, Justin Ryan. I cannot begin to explain the joy I felt as I held him. God gave me a reason to live, to change, to be a better person. I had never laid my eyes on anything more perfect. He was God's gift to me, my little angel. My family surrounded me with love and support and helped me raise this precious bundle of joy.

Things were going very well. I was adjusting to being a mom. I was loving every minute of it. I am convinced that there is no greater human love than a mother's for her child. This gift from heaven had given me a reason to change, and the love that I felt for this small helpless baby was indescribable.

Life was progressing along well, and then I got a call from Jim. He was getting out of jail and wanted another chance at making our family work and to see his son. When Jim finally got out of jail, Justin was three months old. I decided I was going to try and make this work since he was the father of my baby. I knew how the baby had helped me change, so I felt he would be enough to help Jim change as well. Instead, over a short period of time, the physical and emotional abuse began again. I soon found myself back into the cycle of alcohol and drug abuse to numb my feelings. I had relapsed. I left my son with my mother while I was out doing drugs, and when my mother realized what I was up to, she gave me an ultimatum: "I love you but I love this baby more," she said. "If you don't get your life together and get off drugs, I will take you to court and take this baby from you. Your baby does not need to pay for your foolish choices."

I would love to say that I got off drugs and Jim changed and we lived happily ever after, but that was not the case. The physical abuse began to occur more frequently, but this time it was different because my baby could see what was happening to me. The final straw for me came on a particular evening. I was holding Justin as Jim and I began to argue. The argument escalated, and he shoved me back onto the bed. Justin fell out of my arms onto the bed himself, and as I lay there being choked, struggling for my next breath, my son lay there watching this happen. As he and I made eye contact, I promised God: "If you let me live, I will never allow my child to see this happen to me again."

I knew that leaving would not be easy, so I began to plan my getaway. One evening Jim had been drinking pretty heavily, so I told him I wanted us to spend time together, just us two. I took Justin to my mother's house and left him there. I told my mother to pack Justin's bag as I had made plans to go to my aunt's house and stay for about a week while Jim adjusted to the reality of me leaving him. My dad had made an extra key and placed it in a magnetic holder underneath my car so that I would be able to find the key and get away without Jim knowing what I was doing.

As we went back to the apartment that evening, Jim went into a rage, as he normally did when he drank. I found myself on the balcony, refusing to come inside the apartment because I knew what was going to occur. I did not want to get hurt, so I waited for him to get into the shower. After a few minutes, I slipped into the house, went out the front door, ran down the stairs to the car, got my key, and was on my way to my mother's house to pick up Justin. I was so scared that I didn't know what to do. I just wanted to be safe. I left my mother's to head to my aunt's house, where I planned to stay for about a week. From there I would return to my mother's house again after Jim had a chance to cool down and come to the realization that it was over. I left with nothing but the clothes on my back. It was a long week. I desperately longed for a normal life, but the realization of the dysfunction in which I lived pierced my soul. I wanted out. I wanted to change. I had been here many times, but there was something different this time.

Every time I held the precious gift of life in my arms that God had given me, I realized I had to change for him. He deserved it. The prophecy God gave to my mother had come to pass. I now had someone I loved more than Jim who gave me the courage and strength to change, though I knew the road to full healing and recovery would be long.

After a week had passed, I returned to my parents' home, and yes, I went through all the emotions of wanting to get back with Jim. But the fear of what would happen to my baby and me if I did—the fear of my uncertain future—was paralyzing. I felt such an incredible responsibility for my child that I knew I could not go back. Shortly thereafter, Jim returned back to jail, I filed for divorce, and a few months later the divorce was granted. It was then that I finally began to get my life on the right track.

This was a very difficult time in my life. If you have ever experienced a divorce, it is truly like a death. Reality hit: I was twenty years old, divorced, and a single mom. The time of loneliness, grief, and pain were unbearable at times. I sat many times feeling hopeless, staring at the impact of the pain and choices of my past right in the eye. I knew I had someone depending on me to make it, so I just did what I knew to do—give it all to God and start again. Fear became my loyal companion to the point it affected my appetite and sleep. I tried to give it to the Lord and move on, but I felt as if I was in a constant state of panic. I cried out to the Lord many times. Then, one particular evening when I fell asleep, the Lord gave me a dream.

In this dream, I saw my son and myself, my mom, and my grandmother standing in the middle of a road where it seemed the skies had turned black; thunder and lightning was all around us. Suddenly, from out of nowhere, several swirling tornadoes touched down, destroying everything in sight. At that moment we began to look for safety. We saw a church sitting in the near distance and began to run as fast as we could toward it to take shelter. We ran in, shut the door, and made it to the window to see the impact of the storm.

To our dismay, the tornadoes destroyed everything in their path, but they did not come near the church we were in. As I woke up from this dream, I was very troubled. The Lord then began to speak to me and reassure me that as long as I stayed in His will and care, He would protect me from everything that I feared would destroy me. This dream was very impactful on my life and gave me a sense of peace that I can not explain.

As hard as it was, I pushed on with my life. I was doing all I knew to do, but despite my efforts I still suffered the pain of rejection and condemnation from some of those closest to me who refused to give me the benefit of the doubt. Instead, they chose to view me through eyes of judgment, distrust, and their own self-righteousness. It was sometimes overwhelming, enough to make me want to give up, but there was something in me that said, "I don't care what you think or say about me: I know I have changed." I realized that only time would prove to them I was here to stay. God was at work on me. I had begun the healing process.

I began to faithfully go to church, get involved, and make new connections and new friends to occupy my time. I knew I had a long road ahead of me with regard to rebuilding my reputation, but God was with me.

There were times I felt sad because that part of my life was over, but I was also free and hopeful to see where God would lead me. I was very blessed to have the pastor and his wife that I had at the time. Brother and Sister Stanley were an integral part of my healing process.

A few months after I began the healing process, a visiting minister/licensed psychologist came through our church. His name was Dr. James Hughes. He offered counseling sessions to the church members who were in need. I personally think God sent him to New Life Tabernacle just for me. I met with him and received some of the best counsel I have ever received, which I credit, along with the power and strength of God, for helping me make the right choices that began to turn my life around.

I had the habit of looking for people I could help and fix. Those choices had not served me well in my choice of mates thus far. The advice he gave me that changed my life was this: if anyone you will date or are dating reminds you of your past abusers, even in the slightest of ways, RUN!

While that advice may sound very simple, to the point that you might overlook it, it gave me the direction that opened my mindset to give my current husband of almost twenty years, Ken Michael, a shot. Ken and I had just begun talking, and he was nothing like the men in my life who had abused me in my past. In fact, because we were so different, I viewed our relationship as if we didn't have much in common. Dr. Hughes helped me understand that what I perceived as normal was actually abnormal, and the things that I viewed as abnormal or uncomfortable were quite normal. As it was with me, so is it in the life of anyone who has been victim to abuse.

5

THE PATH OF HEALING –
THE JOURNEY BEGINS

Dysfunction becomes your normal, while normal becomes your dysfunction. It's crazy but true. Making the decision to allow someone else into my life was a decision I refused to take lightly. I spent many days and nights in prayer for my future. I knew I would find love again, but I also knew that this time, it had to be God's choice, not my own. I was scared and didn't trust my own judgment to make the right choice. In response to this fear, I gave this over to God, the one whom I did trust, knowing He would direct my footsteps.

At the advice of Dr. Hughes, I began to let my guard down and let Ken in; he stole my heart. He was nonjudgmental of my past, loved me through my pain, supported me through all of life's growing pains, made me laugh in the difficult moments, and gave me the security that every woman desires.

We dated for about fourteen months before we married on March 8, 1996. I was twenty-two years old. In our first year of marriage, God blessed us immensely. Ken was successfully able to adopt Justin as his own, becoming his father. God took the broken pieces of my life, placed them together, and made them whole. My prayer was that God would bless me with a man who would be an incredible father to my son and a husband to myself, so I am living proof today that God answers prayer. Ken was all I prayed for and then some.

During our first year of marriage, the scars of my past began to unravel and played havoc on my mind. It seemed as if every demon from my past that I had tried to lock away all came out at the same time. I truly felt as if I was losing my mind. I had no self-confidence. I trusted no one and was making my husband pay for everything everyone had done to me throughout my lifetime. I was so scared my husband was going to leave me all alone and that I was going to have to start over again. I made myself crazy worrying that he would be unfaithful and I wouldn't be enough. To say the least, I was a wreck.

God gave me the perfect husband when He gave me Ken. He stood by me throughout my healing process. He was there with me through every pain, every tear, every fear, and every worry. He always reassured me he was not going anywhere, that I was all he ever needed. It wasn't fair to him, having to endure what I put him through. I thank God every day that I had sense enough to realize my condition, and after many discussions we decided I should continue the counseling I had started several months prior. I was living in a prison within my own mind, locked in the cold, dark cell of my past. I lived in a constant state of fear that Ken wasn't as good as I thought he was; I was actually waiting for the other shoe to drop to prove to myself that he couldn't love me either. I felt like damaged goods that were being thrown from one place to another. After many counseling sessions, countless prayer meetings, a merciful God, and a wonderful husband who was willing to do whatever it took to see I got the help I needed and the love and support necessary to make it through, I was on the mend. This is a hard step for many because for us to seek counseling for ourselves, we have to admit we are broken. And, as many of us have heard in life, the first step to fixing your problem is to actually admit you have one. It's funny how the first step to our healing is the hardest thing for most of us to do. The path out of our mess generally starts out as just that—messy.

On the path to victory, we must pass through the canals of our broken past, revisiting old scenes of brokenness, fear, and pain. I am so thankful that I let go of my foolish pride and allowed God to place the right people in my life to put me on the right track. My outlook on life was changing. I was able to see things differently. I was going to survive and be victorious.

Life was good. Our home was a house of prayer. We put God first and each other second; this was a new one for me. We shared many wonderful moments as a family. God put us together. It was destiny. My son was being raised in a stable home full of love where he could grow up safe and secure. God was faithful to answer my prayers.

I don't want to make it sound like a fairy tale, that my prince came in on his white horse and whisked me away and we lived happily ever after, because we all know that fairy tales exist only in movies and books. Although my life may not have been a fairy tale, it was a far cry from anything I endured previously; it was heaven to me. The key to the changes that I made in my life rested on two principles. First, I had to take ownership of the mess that I had made of myself. Second, I had to do as the Scripture says, deny myself and follow Him (Luke 9:23). He was now in control. The car of my life finally stayed in its lane when I managed to take my hands off the wheel. What a paradox.

What is it you are going through that looks hopeless? What prayer are you praying for God to answer?

Let me encourage you today. Do not give up. When you think your prayers are falling upon deaf ears, believe me—they are not. God *will* answer.

"Behold, the LORD'S hand is not shortened, that it cannot save;

63

neither his ear heavy, that it cannot hear" (Isa. 59:1).

In 1999, at the age of twenty-five, I began to feel God doing something in me. God placed a burden in my life for souls, a burden to help those in need who were having trouble finding their way. I had such a deep gratitude for what God had done in my life that I wanted to share it with anyone who was going through, or had been through, similar life tragedies as my own.

I remember the night when God spoke to me about working with women who were in need. I was at the altar, praying, responding to a wonderful message preached by evangelist Gordon Poe on reaching for those who are lost. He encouraged the church members to bring those who were hurting and in need of God to a special service our church was having that Friday night. It was called a H.O.P.E. Rally (Healing Opportunities for People Everywhere). I would love to tell you that when God spoke to me, it was a moment that the earth shook and time stood still, but it wasn't. It was just a still, small voice.

You have to understand that after everything I had been through in my life, the very first question I asked God was, "Who am I? How can I help them? I am broken. I am still in need of healing, myself." But it was right then, in the middle of my confessing my inabilities, that I felt the voice of God interrupt me. He didn't let me barter with Him that day. He was calling me to move forward and reach out to the women within my community. In an effort to confirm what I had just heard from God, I told Him: "If this is what you want me to do, tell my husband and he will tell me as well." I did that not believing it would happen. As I got up from the altar and began to walk back to the pew where I was sitting, my husband was walking from the back of the church toward me. Before I could get to the pew to sit down, he stopped me. He said that the Lord had spoken to him, and he felt that we needed to reach out to people within our community and help them. He said he felt an urging in the spirit. At this point, I kind of giggled and told my husband what God had just told me, what I asked God to do in response, really not thinking that he would say to me the very thing God had spoken to me just a few minutes before.

No matter how I wanted to look at it, I knew God was at work. My husband and I stayed around the church, talking with others, until it was almost empty. Our assistant pastor Brent Keating was still in his office, so we stopped by on our way out. We began to tell him what God had just spoken to us. He mentioned that there was a women's rehabilitation facility down the street from our church and that a few people had been trying to get into this facility to minister for a while but had been unsuccessful. He suggested I give it a try, to which I quickly responded yes; God would not let go of me. I went to work the next day, and it seemed as if my lunch hour would never arrive. I had researched the contact information for the woman whom I needed to speak with at the facility. At lunch, I went to my car to give her a call. I have to admit, I was very nervous as I picked up the phone, but I realized the worst thing that could happen is that she could just say no. What would that hurt? I dialed the number, and as the phone began to ring, I was already planning what voicemail I would leave, but to my surprise, she answered. I introduced myself and told her I was with New Life Tabernacle. I explained that we were having a special service that coming Friday night, and that I wanted to see if she would allow me to invite any of the women there who wanted to come.

To my surprise, she quickly approved, and we worked out the details. We would pick them up, feed them dinner afterward, and then take them back to the facility. I have to tell you—when I got off the phone, I was on cloud nine. I began to call everyone, telling them just what God had done. This was the very first door that God opened for me in my ministry; little did I know that He was going to show Himself mightily that Friday night. A really good friend of mine, Rhonda Smith, and I picked up the women that evening and brought them to church. Approximately ten women joined us that evening. The service was filled with excitement, and high expectation was in the air. When we walked into the church, the sanctuary was packed, and all of the women sat toward the back.

The service began with worship. The women enjoyed the music and singing, slowly letting their walls down, opening up to the Lord. As the worship concluded, evangelist Gordon Poe got up and began to preach. As he ministered, faith began to soar. He began giving account of the many miracles and deliverances that God had performed at previous H.O.P.E. rallies and how God told him tonight would be no exception. I'm not sure if words can adequately explain what happened next. As he began to preach and talk about his personal deliverance of overcoming drugs and alcohol, the women stood to their feet; one of them shouted, "Praise the Lord!" You would have had to have been there to fully comprehend the power of God that came into the sanctuary that night. At the very moment that one woman began to speak praises to the Lord, God's Spirit began to minister to her. She began to speak in a heavenly language as God filled her with His Spirit, and just as it happened to her, it began to happen to others. Every woman that came that night walked away as a new creature, filled with the Holy Spirit. The women were baptized that evening, and afterward, Gordon Poe had them come up on the platform to share their experience. Some of them were so overwhelmed by the presence of God, they couldn't even put into words what they had just experienced. I have never felt more alive than I did at that very moment.

Romans 8:28 came to life for me that evening. The Scripture says, "And we know that all things work together for good to them that love God, to them who are the called according to his purpose." God had taken all of my pain and allowed me to be a vessel to help others overcome the same addictions I had struggled with. I felt as if God had reached down from heaven and given me a bear hug. I was so thankful I had listened and obeyed the voice of God. After that evening, my husband and I partnered with Nick and Rhonda Smith and volunteered for several years at the drug rehabilitation center, loving, encouraging, feeding, clothing, and mentoring many of the women there. We baptized women most every

Sunday and watched firsthand as God consistently filled them with His Spirit and transformed their lives. God can do in one moment what man can never achieve in a lifetime. If you are struggling with addiction, it's far too late to tell me that God cannot give you the power to overcome. I experienced it firsthand and have continued to watch God do the same for many others. This was one of the most impactful ministries I have ever been a part of.

After several years of staying faithful to the house of God, working for the Lord and letting the Word of God preached by numerous ministers flood my soul, healing was taking place. When you have been through as many difficult life situations as I have, you must understand healing is a process. It is not instantaneous. I thought I had overcome my past even though there had been many opportunities for a setback, but this one time in particular I allowed the guilt and condemnation of my past to take a toll on me mentally and physically. I had always questioned if I was still using drugs when I became pregnant with my son, and the secret guilt I carried for this was heavy. The Devil knew this and used it against me anytime he could.

When my son was about eight years of age, he began to develop nocturnal seizures. The seizures only occurred at bedtime, when he would go to sleep. His brain struggled transitioning into the deep REM sleep, so it would misfire and throw him into a seizure. Over a period of time, the seizures became more frequent and severe. One evening we took him to the ER, as the seizures were now affecting his sight. After consulting with the ER doctor, we made him an appointment with a neurologist for more extensive testing.

After an EEG and other tests, he was diagnosed with nocturnal seizures and was put on Depakote to control them. This was a long trial. It lasted for a couple of years. All of the fear that I had been delivered from had returned along with past condemnation of mistakes that were under the blood. I allowed this to take its toll on me and my ministry. I now dealt with the fear of him going to school and having a seizure and my husband and I not being there to help him, even though technically there was nothing we could do physically but pray. The medicine changed his personality and had other side effects that mentally tortured me; after all, I blamed myself for his condition.

As we approached the two-year mark of dealing with doctor appointments, EEGs, and the effects of the medication, Justin started having what they call "breakthrough seizures." This was not good news for us as parents because now they were upping the dose on Justin's medication to try and prevent the seizures from occurring. The doctor began to talk to us about the long-term effects, and truthfully, it was terrifying. This road we were walking was trying our faith in God and teaching us to trust Him. But even after the adjustments to the medication, the seizures began to happen again. One evening in particular, Justin experienced one of the worst seizures to date. I remember my husband and I just sat by his bedside, praying and crying out to God as we watched helplessly, wanting to take this from our son but being unable to do much of anything at all. My body shook uncontrollably as it became more than my nerves could bear. My husband, who was my rock, looked at me and said, "Go in the other room and I will stay in here with him." He knew it was more than I could take. As I walked out of the room into my bedroom, I fell to my knees and began to talk to the Lord. I begin to tell the Lord my guilt and shame and everything that I carried and asked Him in His mercy to heal Justin's body.

As I cried to the Lord, He spoke to me and said, "Tomorrow night, when the preacher begins to preach on healing, go up for prayer and I will heal him." We were in revival at our church, and I couldn't wait for the doors to open. I remember the next morning, talking with my son, explaining to him what the Lord spoke to me. I told him, "When the preacher begins to preach tonight, we are going to walk up to the front and God is going to heal you." For a split second, I thought about what other people may think, as my actions were outside the norm of how things were done, but I was desperate for my son's healing, and I would have done whatever the

Lord asked me to do.

That night was a normal church service. As the evangelist got up to minister, he said God spoke to him saying that people would be healed in this service, adding, "And if you need a healing, know that these altars are open." He began preaching his sermon, and I looked at Justin and said, "Are you ready?" He said yes. He grabbed my hand and we walked down to the altar for him to be prayed for. The evangelist asked me what was wrong, and I told him my son needed healing from seizures. He laid hands on him and began to pray. After he prayed for us, he continued preaching while we prayed. After we had prayed a few minutes, we turned around to go to our pew to sit down. The evangelist stopped us and said, "Don't stop. Continue to pray, for the Lord just spoke to me and said He is now going to the source of the problem to complete the healing." We began to pray like never before, and I am thankful to say, and give all glory to God, that Justin never had a seizure again.

During this trial I had many opportunities to allow the Enemy to steal my miracle. I had allowed the Devil to set me back mentally and plague me with guilt and condemnation from my past, but I held on; I didn't quit. Sometimes, just when you think you have overcome some of your past mistakes, the Devil will find a way to use it against you again. Guard yourself, for Satan is as a roaring lion seeking those whom he may devour (1 Pet. 5:8). Don't allow him to steal your faith and discourage you from what God has promised you. He will use every tool available to attack you, but you must stay strong and focused. Trust in God.

In my situation, God had proven Himself faithful once again. He allowed me to see myself as He sees me, through the eyes of love. He delivered me from the guilt and condemnation of my past that I had once again allowed to gain a stronghold on me. God was teaching me valuable lessons of trust and total dependence on Him.

In 2003, my family moved to Frisco, Texas. This brought about many life changes for us. One of the hardest things for us was having to switch places of worship. New Life Tabernacle was so much more than a church: it was family and represented so many healings and victories for us. But despite our lack of understanding, we trusted the Lord.

For a while, we tried different churches closer to home, but nothing seemed to fit until one Sunday morning in July 2004, when we walked into North Cities UPC church, under the leadership of Pastor D. G. Hargrove. When we entered the church that morning, we were desperate for God to give us direction . . . and that He did. As the altar call was given, my husband and I stood at the pew, praying and seeking the face of God. Associate Pastor John Hargrove came up to us; he began to pray over us and even gave us a word of prophecy. We knew, from that moment on, we had found our new home. Nonetheless, we went through a period of adjustment getting to know new people and finding our place within the body of Christ.

During our first year at North Cities, God opened the door for me to become a full-time real estate agent. This was such a blessing to my family. God began to bless us financially as my business grew. I loved helping people, so it was a natural fit for me. My very first year in real estate, I became rookie of the year at RE/MAX Premier Group and quickly had one of the top RE/MAX teams in the Dallas-Fort Worth area . . . until 2010, when the real estate market crashed. Unfortunately, my ambitions and dreams had become self-oriented and not kingdom driven. I had replaced the passion for ministry God had given me for my own dreams. Despite the many times God had dealt with me to come closer and give my life wholly to Him and answer His call, I ignored Him and went about my own life. Frankly, I was having a good time and really didn't have time for anything else. I felt self-sufficient, and although in my mind and with my mouth I was giving God all the glory for my success, my actions spoke otherwise.

After much prayer and consideration, in 2007, my husband and I decided to try and have another child. Our prayers were quickly answered. On September 13, 2008, God blessed us with a beautiful, blonde-haired, blue-eyed, curly-headed girl, just as we had prayed for. She was an answer to prayer and made our family complete.

During this time in my life, my priorities were all messed up; God had taken a backseat to my career. I loved the success I had and the boost it gave to my self-confidence. If there is one thing I have learned in my forty-one years of living, it's that you cannot band-aid issues in your life. You must deal with them head on and work through them, because you can either choose to work through life's hurts and scars on your own, or life will eventually force you to, and that is never fun. When the real estate market crashed in 2010 and business began to dwindle, I found myself in a vulnerable state. This is just where God wanted me. He had a plan for me and saw that I was on a path that would eventually destroy my family and me. Thank God He loved me enough to get my attention.

In my business, the phone stopped ringing, and the homes I had under contract started falling through. There was no money coming in. I no longer felt self-sufficient, and like the prodigal who did things his own way for a while, I woke up in my own pigpen. Thank God I knew where to return, so I went back to the Father's house. I slowed down long enough for God to deal with my heart and found myself drawing closer to God; once again, I found myself battling with the call of God on my life. It was time. God needed me to surrender. I dedicated myself to prayer and fasting because I knew God was dealing with me. I knew I had a choice: I could let go and let God, or I could continue on the self-destructive path I was on. I made the choice to surrender, and over the next few months, God began to work me over. I felt as though God had placed my life back on the Potter's wheel and was remaking my life for His glory.

One morning during prayer, God began to deal with me about the women's ministry at our church, North Cities. God began to speak to me about what He wanted to do there and how He was going to use me to do it. I felt an urge in the spirit to contact my pastor D. G. Hargrove and discuss this with him, so I sent him an email during my prayer time. God wanted me to start monthly meetings for the women of our church to help them grow in relationship not only with Him but also with other women in the church and to help them find their purpose. I knew this was the will of God, so I continued on. Later that day, my pastor contacted me and told me he saw the need and gave me his blessing.

After surrendering to what God wanted me to do, you would think all of the financial hardship we were experiencing would end and everything in my life would be perfect, but that was not the case. I began to battle with my own lack of self-confidence to carry out the call God had placed on my life. I remember standing at the altar one Sunday morning talking to the Lord in response to a passionate message preached by my pastor. I told the Lord I wanted to do what He had called me to do, and if it was truly His will, I asked Him to confirm it. That next week, I worked very hard to find new business while holding together real estate transactions that were falling apart. Real estate is a very stressful career. It can make you feel bipolar. You are on top of the world one moment, because you just put someone under contract, to find yourself under the bus the next when someone's financing falls through or someone changes their mind after you spent all week working with them. It is a very emotional job, especially when you have my personality. I became emotionally attached and involved with every client.

On June 18, 2010, after I asked the Lord to confirm His calling to me, I had two listing appointments and felt confident I would get both. The first appointment was at a home in Plano. The owner of the home lived in California and had asked me to go look at the property and then call him; we would discuss what, if anything, needed to be done to the property to prepare it to be listed and what price it should be listed for. I arrived there at 9:00 a.m. and rang the doorbell. The tenant who answered the door was a little put out because she understood the appointment to be for Saturday, but she let me come in nevertheless. She showed me around the whole house and was pointing things out that needed to be addressed by the seller. I was walking behind her, taking notes, and as we walked into the hallway, headed back to the living room, she suddenly stopped, turned around, and looked at me. I thought she forgot to tell me something.

She just stared at me for a few seconds (which seemed like an eternity) and said, "I don't know if you believe in the gifts of the Spirit or not, and I hope you don't think I'm weird, but God just told me to tell you two things." Of course, I'm thinking, *Oh no, who is this weirdo?* She began to tell me about my son and the ministry that God has called him to, and then she began to tell me to guard my marriage and not let anything come between us. She then told me she could see the pain in my eyes—the pain that I felt as a result of being sexually abused as a child. She talked about the fact that my family had just recently moved into a new home and that there was a lot of turmoil in our home. She told me how I had been deeply betrayed by a close friend and how that my marriage was in disarray.

By this time, I was sobbing. I had never experienced anything like this. This lady did not know me or anything about me, yet she knew my life better than anyone. It then got very quiet, and she looked away. I was thinking to myself, *God why are you allowing her to see so deeply into my life? What is your purpose? Please, reveal it to me.* At that very moment, she looked at me and said, "You just recently asked God to confirm something for you, and He sent me to do so. I am as good as it gets. The ministry that you are entering into will be one of healing for many women. You will help women from all walks of life. You have been very successful in real estate up to this point, but from today on your career will no longer be real estate but just a means to support your ministry." The hairs on my arms stood straight up; chill bumps were all over my body. As she spoke every word, I felt the presence of God; it was as if He embodied Himself in this lady, and I was having a direct conversation with Him.

She then began to talk to me about the future of my ministry, saying, "Within five years, you will write a book." I have to admit that when she spoke about things in my future, my flesh kicked and doubt filled my heart, but I instantly felt convicted for doubting God, seeing what He had just done for me. She and I talked for about fifteen minutes discussing ministry, and she shared that she was a minister at a local church. When it was time to go, we hugged like we were long-lost friends, and she encouraged me to stay strong because God had something special in store for me. I was speechless! (And if you know me at all, that's a condition I'm rarely in. I can talk to a fence post!)

When I got in my car to leave, I just sat in silence, taking in the events that had just occurred. I have to admit, my mind and heart were not into my second listing appointment, but as I was driving to my next appointment, I called my husband to share all that had just happened, and we were both in awe. I told him that when I finished my next appointment, I was going to call Pastor Hargrove and talk to him about what had happened.

I went through the motions of the next listing appointment and was never so glad in all my life to be done. I didn't even get the listing signed, but it didn't matter. I had one thing on my mind and that was to talk with my pastor. That afternoon, I had to go up to the church for something, so I thought I may be able to catch him then. When I got there, the ministry team was finishing up with lunch, and Pastor Hargrove made time to talk with me. As I sat there talking to him, he said he felt that everything she said was on target. I felt a sense of relief coupled with a huge responsibility. It doesn't matter who you talk to: you will find in most everyone's life there is a God moment, and I just had mine. Something was birthed in me that day that I can't explain.

A spiritual boldness overtook me. From that day to this, I have not been the same. I surrendered to the call of God and held the first women's meeting at my home in July 2010. God instructed me to give my testimony and tear down the walls I had built to protect myself. God had a plan. He began to use my past hurts, habits, and failures for His glory. My test was becoming my testimony. That night, God ministered to several women and used my testimony to give them hope and faith for themselves and for their family members.

The most crucial thing we all face is what we are going to do with our lives after we know the direction in which God is taking us. Are we going to be steadfast in faith, holding on to His promises, or are we going to let life's circumstances determine our destiny? God has a calling and a destiny for each of us. He will reveal it to you when you seek Him with your whole heart, withholding nothing, when it is no longer about your agenda, but His agenda. We must get to that place in God where we are so lost in His presence that all we see is Him. God's will and agenda is not about us, but it is about His kingdom, His work.

In May 2011, God began to deal with me about this book, and this book has been a labor of love. A couple of weeks after God spoke to me about this book, my pastor was preaching and said that God told him someone was going to write a book, so they needed to yield and write it! I pray that by sharing my life's story with you and allowing you to see how I overcame the pains of sexual abuse as a child; the physical and emotional abuse in my first marriage; and my experiences of infidelity, divorce, overcoming drug addiction, and hurt and rejection from friends and family, it will show you that God is able. I am not a natural writer, and throughout writing this book I have had many setbacks, but there's one thing I know for certain: God has used the women's ministry called QUEST to breathe hope and fellowship into the lives of the women of North Cities. God has also expanded my ministry to include teaching Celebrate Recovery at our church and helping those in need from various shelters in the community.

My story is one of brokenness, fear, pain, and emptiness. I have no doubt that as you are reading this, your mind has taken you back to things in your own life. Your past—those unhealed wounds that you cannot even bear to think about. God wants to heal those wounds. If you can identify with my story in any way, whether that be in principle or in experience, know God is no respecter of persons. What He has done for me, He will do for you. Are you ready? Then let's talk about it.

PART 2: INTRODUCTION

In the first half of this book, I laid my life open for you. I've shared my pains, shortcomings, and failures, but that is not the purpose of this book in and of itself. What you are about to read is the answer for your brokenness. I believe that the tools and insight, God has given me will help bring you to a place of deliverance and healing. What I will share with you in the next few chapters did not come from a psychology book, but from my personal moments of healing with God Himself. There is a way out. My prayer is to open your eyes to the path of victory that is yours for the taking.

From this moment on, I ask you to do one thing—pull down every wall and allow God to minister to you, healing your brokenness.

These chapters will take a different approach. I want you to know up front that every ounce of my healing process comes back to one key thing, prayer—whether my own prayers in moments of desperation, or when I was so messed up in my own sins that I couldn't pray and someone interceded on my behalf. After reading my story I hope you understand the only reason I am where I am today is because of prayer. So let me start off by saying this before we get into anything else: prayer works.

Even though I have been through a lot, there is a good chance that you may be going through something that I have not. Whether our situations are the same or different, the principles to follow can be applied wherever you are. You can overcome!

6

REMOVE THE MASK

Have you asked yourself one of these questions?

- Who am I?
- Why do I matter?
- What is my purpose?
- What would happen if I lived up to my true potential that God created me for? How would my world be different?

If you are a living, thinking, breathing human being with the capacity to feel pain and hold memory, you have at least asked one of these questions. That is how God designed us—curious and eager. We want to piece together the puzzle of how God created us, why He created us, and why we live under certain circumstances. He gave us complex minds—ones that question, rationalize, and even irrationalize the world around us. Even though God created us with the ability to question, we don't always know the answers. The answers we do know are usually on the surface. Take time to understand where you are and what questions you have for *yourself*.

Where are you in your life today? What keeps you from moving forward? What is weighing you down? Do you hold bitterness, a desire for revenge, or scars from past abuse?

You are the very reason God came to this earth through His Son, Jesus Christ. He took every sin upon Himself at the cross of Calvary and paid the penalty for your sin in full; no debt has been left unpaid. He died so that you might live. He didn't die for you so that you could live a life beat down by shame, guilt, and condemnation. He died so that you could live a life of abundance free from sin, able to fulfill the very purpose He created you for.

"The thief cometh not, but for to steal, and to kill, and to destroy: I am come that they might have life, and that they might have it more abundantly" (John 10:10).

You must learn to separate guilt from shame. There is a difference. You carry guilt when you have done something wrong or made a poor choice. You carry shame when you allow what happened to you to determine your value. You are VALUABLE. God ALWAYS loves the person, but He hates the sin. He separates the two. This is a powerful concept to understand. God NEVER stops loving you.

God created each of us with purpose and value to make us individually unique. You cannot allow life circumstances to dictate who you are. Understanding who you are in God is critical. You cannot internalize your feelings of low self-worth, because this breeds shame . . . and shame will cheat you of your destiny and freedom.

Who are you? Think about this, and once you have a solid answer, live it out in your daily life. It will change the way you talk, the things you do, and the people you associate with. Let today be the first day of the rest of your life. Live intentionally.

It takes work to live life in FREEDOM. The questions you have to ask yourself, ones only you can answer, are "Am I up to the challenge?" and "Do I really want to change?"

"Brethren, I count not myself to have apprehended: but this one thing I do, forgetting those things which are behind, and reaching forth unto those things which are before, I press toward the mark for the prize of the high calling of God in Christ Jesus" (Phil. 3:13–14).

The truth is, if you want to change, you must roll up your sleeves, commit yourself to the often messy healing process, and let nothing stop you: *nothing*. The only person who stands between who you are today and who you can be tomorrow is you; the battle exists within your mind. Fear is paralyzing. Trying to look forward with self-confidence through a lens of our past failures can be quite discouraging, striking us with fear and hindering our journey toward healing. However, the beautiful thing about this journey is we don't have to walk it alone. There is another set of footprints in the sand. There is a God who will walk beside you and me all along the way, "even unto the end of the world . . ." (Matt. 28:20).

We live in a society where it is acceptable to sweep things under the rug because, let's face it, who wants to deal with something painful or uncomfortable? You must recognize right now that this is denial and that your lack of dealing with certain things in your life has halted your progress. It has detoured you from fulfilling your life's purpose. Do yourself a favor and remove the mask you so skillfully hide under. Give God the opportunity He has been waiting for; let Him breathe healing into the very depths of your soul.

One of life's biggest struggles is the uncertainty of our future.

Ask yourself: What are you worried about? Have you allowed worry to consume your life? So many of us spend our days in fear of what tomorrow holds that we miss the very gift that God has given us of today.

How many times have you heard a parent say, "I wish I could go back and relive my child's life over again? I would learn to cherish every moment, worry less, play more, and enjoy every hug like it was the last." "What if" is one of life's greatest thieves. If you are not careful, it can consume you to the point that it begins to affect your health and relationships. What if I had done it this way? What if I had not made that decision? What if? What if is a self-made prison, and somehow, in its penitentiary system, you have managed to become the jailer, judge, watchman, and prisoner, all at the same time. Open the cell door, take ahold of your present, and toss what if into the wind. Yesterday is gone; you cannot get it back. Trying to fix yesterday will thrust you into a cycle of perpetual loss. With no focus on the present moment, today will never be won . . . and tomorrow is granted no hope.

You can say you trust God. Question is, does your life really represent the words you speak? I'm afraid for many of us, the answer would be no. Many of us have heard the saying "talk is cheap." Well, it really is. The old adage "Actions speak louder than words" is such a true statement as well. Can you imagine how God feels when He looks down from heaven and sees you living a life bound by worry? He wants you to surrender every burden and care to Him and trust in His word that all things work together for your good. If you really believed that, you would live your life differently. God's plan is for you to live victoriously through Him. As with any relationship, trust is the foundation. Without trust, there is no frame on which to build a house, no bones on which to build a body, so relationships remain chaotic and formless. So it is in our relationship with God. When you use trust as the measuring stick in your relationship with God, how solid of a relationship do you really have with Him?

This was very eye-opening for me. I thought I was doing okay in my relationship with God, but when I evaluated this one question, I realized I had some work to do. I couldn't worry any longer about tomorrow or about what people may or may not do. Hebrews 13:6 says, "The Lord is my helper, and I will not fear what man shall do unto me."

God is your protector and shield. He will keep you in time of trouble. Are you ready for a big reality check? Worrying is the evidence of your lack of trust in God. In your childhood classes growing up, there was always that one kid who always was a "tattletale." So meet the tattletale of your adult walk with God: *worry*.

You must come to the realization that you are not God. You cannot control the future. You cannot control others. The only thing you can control are the decisions you make from this moment on, and if you choose to put God as Lord of your life and use the Word of God as the blueprint for your life, you can rest assured: your FUTURE IS CERTAIN. A future of hope, joy, peace and love awaits you.

You were not created with the wherewithal to guide your own life. Alone, in your own judgment, you are a lost puppy who has slipped through the fence. The Bible puts it to us in different terms in Isaiah 53:6, "All we like sheep have gone astray . . ."

In Scripture we are often illustrated as sheep, with the Lord as our Shepherd. Have you ever seen a sheep that could lead itself? Likely you have not. There is high relevance in this scriptural comparison to us as sheep. The reality is, sheep have no defense mechanisms to spare them from the dangers that exist along their journey. They are vulnerable, they lack direction, and when the Shepherd is absent, chaos quickly ensues. Like sheep, not only do you need the Shepherd, but also you need other sheep. Never underestimate the power of godly fellowship.

If you choose to sit back and reject God, continuing to play the role of the Shepherd in your life, you have a future that is certain. It is a future filled with pain, guilt, shame, and condemnation. It is a future filled with carrying the weight of the world, which you as a human being were not created to carry. The decision is yours. Who will be God of your life, you or the Creator of the universe, God Himself? I know you have chosen to make God the Lord of your life. I believe that with all my heart. You want to change, but somehow feel trapped and don't know how or where to start. I am here to share with you the very things God has shown me as I embraced the process of healing in my own life. I am not here to tell you that the journey will be easy, but I am here to tell you from experience, it is worth it.

DON'T LET YOUR PAST OR WHAT WAS DONE
TO YOU BECOME YOUR IDENTITY.

You may find yourself resisting the challenge to change because of the pain of your past, the fear of the unknown, and your inability to believe that you deserve a better life. I am here to speak life into you. *By the power of the name of Jesus Christ, I come against every destructive belief system that plagues your mind and keeps you bound with feelings of inadequacy and fear. You will break free from every chain that has you bound and begin to LIVE, truly LIVE.*

God loves you, and it is not His will that you suffer. He is waiting for you to take the first step of surrender, and He will meet you there. God wants to make you new. He wants to put you on the Potter's wheel and remove the scars of your past. God sees every scar, every wound, even those you try to hide. But you should first understand you can hide your hurts from your friends and family, but you can't hide them from your Creator. Is there something you are trying to hide and need to surrender to God?

What are you hiding behind your mask? It is time for you to remove the mask, be honest with yourself, and stop making excuses. Honesty is truly the best policy. Some of the wisest words I have ever heard come from my pastor, D. G. Hargrove. He says this about honesty: "The greatest gift that you can give yourself is the gift of self-honesty." When you do this, you are taking the first step and allowing God to begin a work in you that only He can do. What does the word honesty mean? It means "free of deceit and untruthfulness, to be truly sincere." That is exactly what you have to be if you want to find true healing and freedom in your life. Honesty can sometimes be painful. It reveals things about yourself that you sometimes don't want to see or are not ready to deal with.

It's important that you stop making excuses. Realize that you have tried to control things on your own to avoid being hurt, only to find yourself lost, alone, and feeling hopeless. This is not a fun place to be. I have been there. I remember thinking, *I can't do this anymore; I need help.* Have you ever felt as though you were in a self-destructive pattern and didn't know how to get out of it? If you have, you are not alone. There have been times that I knew I was making a poor choice, but I felt as though I couldn't help myself.

Do you think this is what Paul meant when he said in Romans 7:18, "For I know that in me (that is, in my flesh,) dwelleth no good thing: for to will is present with me; but how to perform that which is good I find not"? I think this was a moment of self-reflection for Paul. He realized there is no good thing in him and that without God, he does not have the power to do good. You must do the same. You cannot skip this step in the process of healing. You need help. You need a spiritual transformation. Paul experienced this on the road to Damascus, and from that very moment, his life changed. We need more than just words. We need an **EXPERIENCE**.

When you look at Paul's life and the evil he did prior to his spiritual transformation, it's easy to think, *He is too far gone. God can't use him.* Well, that is a lie. It doesn't matter where you have been or what sin you have committed. God is waiting with open arms to welcome you home. *In the name of Jesus, I bind the spirit of condemnation that imprisons you and loose spiritual freedom in your life from this moment on.*

Believe me, it is not out of your reach; you can have it if you want it. How? It's easy. Don't complicate the process of living *for* God. All you need to do is SURRENDER and admit your need for God and follow Him. It's really just that easy. See, God wants TOTAL SURRENDER. He doesn't want you to pick and choose which parts of your life you give Him. He wants all of you, withholding nothing. Total surrender is a struggle for all of us. Whether you want to admit it or not, we all love being in control. You can surrender now or wait until you have made a bigger mess out of your life and surrender then . . . it's really up to you.

Yeah, but I don't want to give up everything and allow someone to control my life, some might be thinking. Understand you will always be a slave to something. You will either be a slave to sin or a slave to God. I know from experience that drug addicts want to be free, but instead they are enslaved by the power the drug has over them. That is why a drug addict cheats, steals, and kills to get the next fix. It's not them. It's the power they are allowing to control them. You will either be a force for good or for evil. *You* decide!

Sometimes we don't want to give up control to God because we are afraid of what He will take from us. I can honestly say God never took anything from me that He did not replace with something of greater value. And while I am on the subject of drugs, let me say a couple of things.

When someone is addicted to drugs and is in an endless cycle of recovery, DON'T EVER write them off as hopeless. As long as there is breath in their body, there is hope. You must not confuse someone who is in their despair with who they really are. Most addicts are where they are because they have underlying issues that cause them pain, and this is their way of escape. I am not saying we should excuse their poor choices and behavior, but we need to look at them through eyes of compassion, pray for them, and be there to support them.

Stop trying to control everything and act as if you have it all together. No one does. I don't care who you are. You struggle with something. Some people are just better than others at masking it. We are all in a spiritual battle. Ephesians 6:12 says, "For we wrestle not against flesh and blood, but against principalities, against powers, against the rulers of the darkness of this world, against spiritual wickedness in high places."

As I began to study the word "wrestle," I looked back to the Greek definition. The Greek word for wrestle is palē. It means "To struggle; to wrestle; to fight against, grapple, scuffle, tussle." In Paul's day, the victor of a Greek wrestling match was the one who could hold the other opponent down and gouge their eyes out, leaving them in blindness for the rest of their life. The loss to the opponent was great. Now you see the context of the word "wrestle" in Paul's day as he is writing. I hope you can see the seriousness of the battle you are in. Physical blindness is bad, but spiritual blindness is much worse. Your soul is at stake. May God open your eyes so that you can see yourself for who you are but, most of all, as He sees you. You are valuable. God loves you.

Let's look a little deeper into spiritual transformation. I have already said that the first step is surrender. You must recognize your need for help and realize your need for God.

Remember, spiritual transformation is a process, so don't worry how it will happen; you do your part and God will do the rest. Repentance is the next step. And what is repentance? True repentance is more than an initial prayer confessing your sins to God and asking for forgiveness, although that is absolutely necessary. It's not just a one-time thing; it is something you must do daily. It is a change of lifestyle. It is a turning point in your life where you turn your back on sin and make a change in your life to follow God. It's dying to the old you. Remember, the Bible says, "Therefore if any man be in Christ, he is a new creature: old things are passed away; behold, all things are become new" (2 Cor. 5:17).

After you repent, DON'T STOP!!! God has so much more for you. He wants to fill you with His Spirit. When this happens, you are given a new DNA. You have a new identity in Christ. You are set apart for His purpose. God has a plan for you much bigger than you can see. Remember, you are not in this alone. You have joined forces with the Master of the universe.

A MOMENT OF REFLECTION

QUESTIONS

- Who am I and why do I matter?

_____

_____

_____

- Where am I in life today?

_____

_____

_____

- What would happen if I lived up to my true potential in God, and how would my world be different?

_____

_____

_____

- What am I hiding behind my mask?

_____

_____

_____

- If I were truly free, what would that mean for me?

_____

_____

_____

7

PREPARE FOR BATTLE

As I was writing this book, my husband began to take a keen interest in the Navy SEALs. The more he read, the more their principles applied to my book. One of those principles was the way a SEAL trains. Only a small percentage of candidates ever make it through the grueling conditioning to become a Navy SEAL. The candidates would sometimes grow to despise their brutal trainers. It was hard for them to understand why they had to train so hard. It made no sense . . . until they found themselves in the battle of their lives. An unprepared soldier wilts in battle, but when you've properly trained, it's not overwhelming. When we've put in so much effort in training, the battle will pale in comparison. There is a strong confidence in preparedness. That's why SEALs train until no one can execute better.

When my husband was telling me this, I began to think about how much trust is involved on the SEAL's part with their officers. Throughout their training, they really don't comprehend why they are pushed so hard. They don't fully understand until it is time for them to fulfill their purpose. Then it all becomes clear, and any distain they may have had for their training officer turns to gratitude. How true is that in our own lives? We spend so much of our time angry at God, thinking, *If He loved me, why did all of these things happen to me?* We carry these feelings until we are able to save someone we love with advice only we can give because of the trials we have endured. It is then, at that moment, the Scriptures take shape and we see through the eyes of God and begin to understand. Because we remained faithful, we have stepped into our purpose and didn't even realize it. Trusting in the character of God is crucial for us to continue walking this journey with Him, particularly when life throws us a curveball, and we don't understand why. How can you trust in God when a mountain of negative thoughts rush into your mind like an avalanche? When that familiar feeling of fear creeps in? You simply choose to trust God. It's a choice.

So many people miss out on the blessings of God because they have a distorted view of whom He is. Unfortunately, the situations we face help define our view of God. He is a God of love, grace, and mercy. He is gracious and kind, a gentleman who will never force Himself on you. He is always with you. When you are walking in the valley or standing on the mountaintop, He is by your side. When we understand who God is and see a true picture of God's love for us, then we can experience HOPE for a new future.

In Luke 15:12 the prodigal son says, "Father, give me the portions of goods that falleth to me . . ." Notice he did not say "please" or "may I have?" He knew he was his father's child and wanted access to his inheritance. He gave little or no thought of how this would affect his father emotionally or financially. This young man was what we would describe as arrogant, selfish, heartless, and stubborn. True, it was his inheritance, but his father was not yet dead. The money was his, but he wanted it before its time. He had no right to it when he asked. It was his father's to control as he saw fit, but the Bible says he gave him the portion of his inheritance. The young man left and wasted it on riotous living.

Notice the father gave the son the freedom and possessions he desired so that he could live his life as he chose. Then, after a period of time, he had exhausted his inheritance and found himself feeding swine in a pigpen. The Bible says he came to himself, and when he did, all of the poor decisions he made in an effort to please himself and take control of his life came crashing down. In that moment, his mind went back to the life he lived in his father's care. He thought to himself, *Even the hired servants at my father's house have enough bread to eat. I will return home and request that I be made one of his hired servants.* In his mind, he was no longer worthy to be called his son. This is the mindset that can sometimes hinder our own progress.

Our mistakes keep us from returning to God for help. We no longer see ourselves as a son or daughter, but something the Father would no longer even want. The Bible says the father saw his son returning from a long way off. That means the father was looking for his return. (And that's the picture you need to have of your heavenly Father.) The father greeted him with a hug and kiss. He asked the servants to get the best robe for him to wear and put a ring on his hand and shoes on his feet. The father didn't waste time condemning him of his wrong. Instead, he threw a party in celebration of his son's return home. This is just like our God. God's love is unfailing. He is not waiting to beat us up when we fall or make a wrong choice. Instead, He is here to help, uplift, encourage, and heal us. The story of the life of the prodigal son is such a beautiful portrayal of the unending love and mercy of God.

I spent so much of my life living with a misconception about God that it affected how I viewed Him. I lived in condemnation rather than in hope for a brighter tomorrow. Condemnation closed the door to any possibility of growth for me, but when my eyes were opened and I began to see God for who He is, thanksgiving and hope began to flood my soul. No matter how deep in sin I was, He was waiting for me in anticipation for my return home. You must understand the difference between condemnation and conviction. Many get these two confused.

Condemnation is a tool of the Enemy used to bring up past sins and make you so ashamed that you isolate yourself from people and God because you feel unworthy. Conviction, on the other hand, is the loving hand of God that opens your eyes and heart to see yourself in your sinful state and moves you to run to Him in repentance. Condemnation makes you run *from* God, where conviction draws you *to* God. So the next time the Devil comes against you, making you feel ashamed and unworthy for your past that you have given to God, understand that this is a trick and quote the Scripture below.

"There is therefore now no condemnation to them which are in Christ Jesus, who walk not after the flesh, but after the Spirit" (Rom. 8:1).

From this moment forward, may God open your eyes to view yourself as He sees you. May the guilt and condemnation from past hurts and mistakes be removed by the power of the name of Jesus and replaced with the spiritual freedom God has for you. You are a child of the King, and from today on, may you begin to embrace the life He has for you. There is hope, and it is only found through our Lord and Savior, Jesus Christ. When you come to yourself as the prodigal son did and give God control, you will look back and realize it was the most impactful decision you ever made for yourself.

This doesn't mean you will live a life free from hurt, pain, or bad decision-making. But when those things happen, you will not go down that familiar, destructive path. You will allow those situations to mold and shape you into the man or woman of God He has chosen you to be. You will become better, not bitter. It is God living within you that gives you the strength and power to change, forgive, and move forward. You cannot do this alone. I know I couldn't. If you are honest with yourself, you know you can't either.

It's amazing that when you understand the character of God, you realize He cannot lie. If His Word says it, it is TRUTH. If He promises it to you, it will come to pass. His Word is "forever . . . settled in heaven" (Ps. 119:89). When you anchor yourself to this truth, you will begin to expect the miraculous in your life. Remember the words of Paul in Philippians 1:6 that say, "Being confident of this very thing, that he which hath begun a good work in you will perform it until the day of Jesus Christ."

Don't let your confidence in God be shaken. Men will fail you, but God will never fail you. Every man has been given a measure of faith, and if you will exercise your faith and trust in God, you will begin to be transformed into a new creature. Through His Spirit, God will give you the power and the strength to face your fears and accept yourself, flaws and all.

"For I say, through the grace given unto me, to every man that is among you, not to think of himself more highly than he ought to think; but to think soberly, according as God hath dealt to every man the measure of faith" (Rom. 12:3).

In our lives, if we are not careful, we can go into battle ill equipped and ill prepared. Satan will not fight fair. He will look for every advantage he can find. Know this: he studies you. How do you fight an adversary you do not understand? A soldier would never go into battle with weapons he has not trained with. In 1 Samuel, we find that David had been anointed king while he was only a little shepherd boy. It would be years before he ascended to the throne. He first had to go through some training. It was during his time as a shepherd that he trained for his greatest battle. He didn't know it was training, but it was.

One night while David was watching over his father's sheep, a bear came to take one. David killed the bear. Later a lion tested David again, but the results were the same. David understood the tactics of his enemy. It was only one little lamb. He had many. If he lost one, what difference would it make? David knew if he allowed the lion or the bear to take one, they would not be satisfied. They would return for another. (Note that we sometimes look at what the Devil wants and think, *That's not much; it's not a great loss.* At some point, you will have to take a stand and fight. Satan will take everything you have, one little lamb at a time.) Around this time, David was sent to check on his older brothers, who were in battle. As he approached the valley, a booming voice was heard. It was a challenge from Goliath. The armies of Israel cowered in fear. Can you blame them? Goliath stood around nine feet tall. The head of his spear weighed fifteen pounds. Who could deal with that? Yet when David heard his challenge, it was a call to battle. He wanted to fight the giant. The king gave David his own shield, sword, and armor, but David said, "I've not tried these." He had never gone into battle with those weapons. Instead, he stepped out with what he had trained with, a sling and a name. The Bible says that David ran to meet Goliath. A properly trained soldier is prepared to fight. David was ready, trained, and he trusted God.

To prepare yourself, you must dig into the Word of God and spend time in prayer for not only your salvation but also for direction and the principles of healing. You must be willing to let go and trust the God that created you and submit to the process. How badly do you want your healing? You cannot shortcut the process. So many people want out, but don't want to put in the time or the training. They want a magic pill. But life does not work that way. If you try to shortcut the healing process, you will be ill equipped, and in the heat of battle, you will be an easy target. Your destruction will be imminent. You have to educate yourself with the proper tools to defeat your adversary. It's one thing to understand the tools you need to effectively fight a battle, but it's a different story to know how to use them. How do you know how to use the tools God has given you unless you put them into use? I dislike trials as much as the next person, but it is through our trials that God perfects us. He is working out all of our imperfections and purifying us in an effort to make us more like Him. He breaks down the wall of resistance and self-reliance until we cry out to Him, "I can't do this without you."

Sometimes, everyday life will sink people, drive them from God, and become a stumbling block. Even when bad things happen, you can make up in your mind to learn and grow from them, knowing that God has a greater plan.

Things are going to happen to us all. This battle we are in is called life. But sometimes we are ill prepared because we don't want to put in the time or effort to train, so we are not prepared for the fight. When you make contact with the Enemy, shots will be fired at you. Unfortunately, there are times when a wound is inflicted. Sometimes we are even wounded by friendly fire.

When Job was going through his trial, his friends thought they were being helpful. They told him, "It it must be your fault. You did something wrong." Their intentions may have been good, but the words were nonetheless hurtful. A wound is a wound. Your body does not care how it was inflicted. It only knows it was wounded. When you are ill equipped and not using the Word of God as your blueprint for living, you open yourself up as an easy target for the Devil. Paul refers to us as soldiers and admonishes us in Ephesians 6:10–18 by saying, "Finally, my brethren, be strong in the Lord, and in the power of his might. Put on the whole armour of God, that ye may be able to stand against the wiles of the devil. For we wrestle not against flesh and blood, but against principalities, against powers, against the rulers of the darkness of this world, against spiritual wickedness in high places. Wherefore take unto you the whole armour of God, that ye may be able to withstand in the evil day, and having done all, to stand. Stand therefore, having your loins girt about with truth, and having on the breastplate of righteousness; And your feet shod with the preparation of the gospel of peace; Above all, taking the shield of faith, wherewith ye shall be able to quench all the fiery darts of the wicked. And take the helmet of salvation, and the sword of the Spirit, which is the word of God: Praying always with all prayer and supplication in the Spirit, and watching thereunto with all perseverance and supplication for all saints."

These Scriptures are powerful. The Scriptures tell us who our enemy is: the Devil. Scripture teaches us our battle is not against flesh and blood, but against spiritual wickedness in high places. What I love most is that it doesn't leave us feeling defeated, because Paul gives us a solid plan for victory. He tells us how to be a good soldier and put on the armor of God, and when we feel we have done all we can to fight our adversary, he admonishes us to just stand. Stand and continually pray so God can fight our battle for us. Why does Paul tell us to put on the whole armor of God? Without putting on the helmet of salvation, you open up your mind to attacks. We all know this is the biggest and most challenging battle we will face. Our mindset is huge. It will determine how we respond to life's challenges and how we come out on the other side. The breastplate of righteousness protects our heart from unforgiveness, offense, and wounds. It allows us to protect ourselves from a root of bitterness and won't allow anything harmful to our spirit to take root. The belt of truth will protect us from the persuasion of this new age culture. It will keep us firmly grounded on the one true foundation, and that is Jesus Christ. You will be solid and unmoveable by life's circumstances and peer pressure. You will be able to stand when no one else can.

The shield of faith is crucial to battle so that you may be able to deflect the fiery darts of the wicked and prevent them from ever making contact. It's important you guard yourself so that you are not overcome by your carnal desires and temptations.

The shoes of peace are important because they give us good footing and prevent backsliding. You never want to remove your shoes during battle because when the terrain gets rough, you will need them to help hold you steady to prevent falls. All five pieces of the armor I have described to you are defensive in nature and crucial to your safety.

Now let's talk about the only offensive weapon that God has given us. It's the sword of the Spirit, which is the Word of God. Satan tried to tempt Jesus Himself in the wilderness after He had been fasting forty days and nights. Every time Satan tempted Him, Jesus said these three words, "IT IS WRITTEN." Jesus used the Word of God as His offensive weapon to force Satan to flee. If we as Christians could understand the value of this one offensive weapon and put it to use, we would all live a victorious life. I compare many Christians to a soldier who is heading out to battle, but doesn't take his weapons to protect himself. We would all say that is absurd, but that's what we often do. Remember that a careless action of a soldier puts himself and those around him in danger. It is critical to understand you are in battle. You must equip yourself daily so that you can protect yourself as well as the family which God has blessed you with.

I love how Paul closes out these few verses. He tells us how to arm ourselves and then talks to us about staying in an attitude of prayer and watchfulness so that the Enemy does not take us unaware. You must become like a SEAL, highly trained and prepared for battle. If you don't take time to equip yourself, life will offend you. You will fight bitterness, jealousy, guilt and shame. When I look at everything I have been through in my life, both good and bad, I see how Scripture has come to life. For example, Romans 8:28 says, "And we know that all things work together for good to them that love God, to them who are the called according to his purpose."

I have asked, "Why me?" only to see years later how that one experience enabled me to help someone who was suicidal or hopeless. I can now say with confidence what God did for me; it allows me to lead others to the cross so God can administer the same healing to them. Let's face it, people who are dealing with these crisis issues don't feel comfortable talking to someone who cannot relate to them. It's just words to them. The last thing they need is for someone to just feel sorry for them and make them feel more like a victim. They need someone who can say, "I was there," someone who can relate. In life, you may have found yourself a victim, but now, by the help and grace of God, you will be a victor.

A MOMENT OF REFLECTION

QUESTIONS

• Do I explicitly trust God with my life?

_____

_____

_____

• How have I allowed condemnation to hinder my progress?

_____

_____

_____

• What battle am I facing?

_____

_____

_____

• What things have I allowed the Enemy to steal from my life?

_____

_____

_____

• Have I armed and trained myself for battle? If not, in what areas am I lacking?

_____

_____

_____

8

THE WOUNDS

What happens when you are wounded in battle? If left untreated, your wounds may become fatal. When you enter a battle, no one plans to get hurt, but sometimes, through no fault of our own, wounds happen. Do you have infectious wounds that have been left untreated?

I had an infectious wound from my drug abuse. It was so bad that my arm had swollen to three times its normal size. It looked as though it would explode. The danger was if the infection was not contained, it would get into my bloodstream and kill me. So the doctor performed emergency surgery to clean out all of the infection. I was left with a deep open wound in my arm that was packed with gauze. It was painful, but the process was necessary for me to heal. The wound had to heal from the inside out. The reality was, my physical wound was visible, so it had to be addressed. But the most deadly wound I had was internal, and no one knew. Because we can hide our internal wounds, we don't properly deal with them. They become wounds that never heal. They often affect our physical and mental health and can spiritually kill us.

If I would have just covered the wound with a band-aid, it would have killed me. Because it was left untreated, it started affecting my health. It forced me to address it. I began to feel physically ill and feverish. The doctor pumped antibiotics through my blood to address the physical wound on my arm that was keeping my whole body from functioning properly.

There will come a time in your life that you will have to deal with those difficult life issues that weigh you down. You must stop sweeping them under the rug. This is a very painful process. I was forced to deal with the infection in my arm. The process of removing the infection left me in excruciating pain. I lost use and function of my right arm in the healing process. Once it began to heal, I had to go through therapy to get full mobility of my arm again. If I would have quit before I went through therapy, I would have lost the full use of my arm. It would have never returned to its full function or operated at its full ability God intended for it to have.

When something happens to us, we want the healing, but we don't want to go through the painful process of therapy. We stop short, so our full mobility is stunted and we can't be used to our fullest potential in Christ. When you have an emotional wound, it affects other things. Just like a physical wound, it may start off small—perhaps as a little cut—but if not treated properly, infection can set in so severely that the area of infection doesn't receive proper blood supply. That often leads to gangrene, which can be debilitating.

Think of it this way: when you have an emotional wound you choose not to address, you begin to build up walls between you, others, and God. You are essentially cutting yourself off from the direct blood flow of Jesus Christ to your life, and we all know that without proper blood supply, spiritual gangrene will set in. You will find yourself spiritually debilitated, lost, without purpose. If there is anything I want to convey to you, it's the importance of dealing with internal pain and emotional wounds. You can't keep that mask on forever. It will bleed into other areas of your life and leave you feeling hopeless. For example, you can't have a sexual abuse wound and it not affect another area of your life in some way. It affects your relationships and your ability to accept love from others.

As a woman who suffered years of sexual abuse as a child, let me say this: "Don't be ashamed, get help!" Today's culture is filled with all sorts of media playing to the sexual desires of men and women. In advertising, let's face it: sex sells. Being a victim of sexual abuse, I can honestly say that the effects of it are felt for a lifetime. I am here today to share the aftermath of such abuse so that others can find strength and healing to move on and begin to truly live a life that is free from fear and hate, a life of purpose.

Suffering from sexual abuse left me feeling cheap, humiliated, and dirty. God did not intend for us to feel this way, but because we live in a world full of sin, we unfortunately have to deal with its outcome. Sexual abuse is a topic that is not discussed in most settings. It is looked upon as a taboo subject that many are fearful to address. Why? The only conclusion I can come up with is that we all know someone who has been abused—or is the abuser. We don't understand the dynamics involved, so we choose not to address it. It's too painful or maybe even disgraceful for some, so it's better to just keep quiet and let the pieces fall where they may. For me, finally speaking out about what happened evoked many mixed emotions. I am just like every other person who wanted to sweep those horrible memories and feelings under a rug and act as if it never happened. I didn't want to be known as a victim. But the truth is, I was a victim; I just chose not to stay there. Are you going to remain a victim or become a victor?

I know what it's like to live in a prison of fear because of the unmentionable acts of another human being trying to achieve sexual gratification. It is a place that I hope no one is in, but I know that many are. Fear is a very powerful thing: it makes people act in ways they never thought they would and say things they can't take back. When sexual abuse is ongoing, it truly becomes a life of hell. You never know when you can let your guard down and just relax. You always have to live with your guard up. You begin to try and reason with yourself to figure out what you have done or are doing to bring this upon yourself, but let me make this clear: You don't have to do anything to be sexually abused. It's not your fault.

People who have a sexual addiction will do whatever it takes to fulfill their desires, and frankly, they don't care who they hurt. A sexually abused child does not know how to make it stop. I know this because I had lived my whole life trying to erase this bad memory. You do well for a while, but at different stages in your life, particularly when you have kids, those feelings of insecurity flood your mind as you strive to protect your children and ensure they never have to experience the shame of sexual abuse as you did. You begin to psychoanalyze everyone and find yourself back in the same prison you thought you had escaped. I can't explain the feelings of anger and hatred you may feel. You have been robbed of those carefree days of youth that you watch others enjoy. For me it created a feeling of jealousy and resentment that I had to deal with. It's hard to explain the human mind and why we think the way we do, but when you grow up with abuse, in some sick way that life style is normal. Victims don't know life any other way. You want to be happy and secure, but you are too embarrassed and ashamed to speak out and seek the help you need so you can begin to heal.

People who are abused can be some of the greatest actors you will ever meet. They live as though life is perfect on the outside. The funny thing is, they become so good at this that people actually want to be them. Isn't that ironic? When you are going through this alone and you don't get help, I know the lonely, sad nights you experience. This place in life is a very dark moment, and for many it will be a crossroads. The decisions you make here will determine your destiny. You don't have to stay a victim. You can overcome this nightmare and live in total freedom.

I understand why some people who experience abuse keep silent. They believe this information will devastate the ones they love the most. They don't know how their loved ones will react and are afraid of losing the only love and security they truly feel.

When I was seventeen years old, I remember speaking out about my abuse. It was done in a very rebellious way, and not for the right reasons, but nonetheless, I spoke out. The effects of it were painful, but over time I found healing.

I remember when my son, Justin, was at the same young age when sexual abuse entered my life. That's when I began dealing with the mental repercussions of my abuse. I felt it was my purpose to ensure he never experienced the pain that I did. All the feelings of helplessness, anger, frustration, insecurity, and fear resurfaced with a vengance. It finally set in: Not only had the abuser robbed my childhood, but I wasn't able to enjoy my son's childhood the way I should have. I was dealing with the same feelings, but in a different light.

As I sat there looking at the innocence of my child, I began to feel a "momma bear" instinct come over me like never before. It was as if I was daring someone to hurt him. It had made me into a very overprotective mom who went above and beyond to ensure her children didn't experience any kind of pain.

As a young child, I lacked the wisdom to comprehend why God would allow this to happen. At that time, I had not been exposed to the concept of God's will and man's will. I didn't realize God made us all with a free will of choice. By doing this, God gave us a beautiful freedom, but with that freedom also came a negative side, and that is man's will when acting outside of God's Word. When man chooses to make poor choices that don't please God, it unfortunately hurts not only that individual but also the life of the victim as well. Although this understanding eluded me, God gave me the strength I needed to get through it. God gave me a peaceful knowledge that He was there, and I had some great people in my life who loved me and nurtured me through a trying time they knew nothing about. Now, at forty-one, I have a level of understanding that I didn't have before. Now I can see the master plan of God unfolding in my life.

Being sexually abused left me feeling like I couldn't trust anyone. I became a control freak and had to control everything about
my life in an effort to protect myself. This need for control had a
downside. When I felt control slipping away, it was replaced with
a feeling of chaos. It seemed as though I was spinning in the wind,
desperately looking for anything to grab, something to stabilize my
life. This one thing has hindered me so much in my walk with God
and even in the writing of this book. I know what God has spoken
into my life and the many great things He has in store for my future. I just had to relinquish all control to God and trust in Him so
He could do His work.

Relinquishing control is a huge issue for people who have been
abused. They have the tendency to become controlling people. It's
not their personality. It's simply a protective mechanism. But the
problem with this hypervigilant reponse is this: when you are a
victim and you use this mechanism of control, you eventually find
yourself living in your own prison. Don't allow this prison to become a life sentence.

Know that you can go through any self-help book or program,
but if you are not applying the principles of the Word of God and
bathing your life in prayer, you will struggle. We all try to fix our
own problems, the devastating issues that come our way. We can
not do this alone. It is only by the power of God that you'll have the
strength to overcome. I want you to understand the reality of what
you have been through. I don't want to leave you with a misconception that your past will never bother you again, because that is not
true. You will have triggers for the rest of your life that will bring
back haunting memories of things you have been through. Triggers
aren't always bad. They help us know where we are in the healing
process. Sometimes these triggered memories require another trip
through the healing process. How do you do that? You must continually keep giving it back to God.

How do you give it back to God? You do it in a healthy manner, and not in an intentional self-destructive pattern of alcohol and drugs to numb the pain. You take it through the right channel, which means you have an honest conversation with God. You lay it all out there by pouring out your heart to the Lord. If you have prayed about something and feel you have given it to God and are still struggling with the aftermath of your past, God has given you the body of Christ for you to find support and healing. It's okay to go to a CHRISTIAN counselor/leader in the church who can help guide you through the process of what the Word of God says. Sometimes we need someone to help us see things in a different light, through the lens of God's Word. While in battle, you are so busy fighting to survive that you can't see the big picture. You can't see that if you keep fighting, you are almost home. You don't realize that you're about to make it. You can't see you are approaching your God-given destiny—the next level of healing that God has ordained for you.

If you are not careful, you can get so weary in this intense battle that you give up just before the finish line. And when you give up, the Enemy, your adversary, is waiting to finish you off. The trials that come at you in life are meant to wear you down both mentally and physically. Every self-help book talks about denial, forgiveness, etc., and all of those things are crucial. I don't want to minimize them, but I do want to talk to you about the day-in, day-out battle for your soul.

Satan is waging war. We talked earlier about how the most challenging battle you will fight is in your mind. You cannot allow condemnation and your distorted view of life and others to isolate you, to convince you that you are done. You don't fit in anymore. You are damaged goods, etc. Your actions may have even caused harm to others, but once you have confessed your sins to God and asked forgiveness, you have to shake off the guilt and shame and move on. You have to stand up and with boldness declare you are a blood-bought child of the King to break the chains of oppression and depression that have been sent for your destruction. You are valuable. It may be that every morning for a while you have to pick yourself up out of bed, wash your face, and look in the mirror and declare who you are in God. Words are powerful.

Because of the scars from the sexual, physical, and emotional abuse plus the self-inflicted wounds of addiction, I was plagued with low self-esteem, shame, guilt, and condemnation.

Those things happened to me, but I made the decision to be a victor and not a victim: I OVERCAME.

"But we have this treasure in earthen vessels, that the excellency of the power may be of God, and not of us. *We are* troubled on every side yet not distressed; *we are* perplexed, but not in despair; persecuted, but not forsaken; cast down, but not destroyed" (2 Cor. 4:7–9).

When you have a made-up mind to become the victor instead of the victim, you will do whatever it takes, and you too will over-come. There is healing and freedom in complete submission to God. You can be free from the cycle of numbing your pain through self-destructive actions, drugs, and alcohol. You now understand the healthy way to deal with your problems, and instead of carrying them yourself, you lay them at the foot of the cross.

You now know how to handle the battles of life. When you get depressed, you don't go looking for a fix to numb the pain. You take it to God and deal with your pain in a healthy manner. YOU ARE A VICTOR!!!

A MOMENT OF REFLECTION

_____

_____

_____

_____

_____

_____

_____

_____

_____

_____

_____

_____

_____

_____

_____

_____

_____

_____

_____

QUESTIONS

• What wounds am I trying to hide?

_____

_____

_____

• Have my wounds been properly treated?

_____

_____

_____

• What walls have I built up that need to come down?

_____

_____

_____

• Do I have issues relinquinshing control of my life to God? If so, in what ways?

_____

_____

_____

• Am I living my life as a victim or a victor?

_____

_____

_____

9

OVERCOMING THE UNSEEN AND UNFORESEEN ENEMY

The Bible declares that God created man and placed him in the garden. He was the keeper of the garden. God saw that man needed a helper and created woman out of the man. The garden and man were in perfect balance. Perfect harmony. The lion would lay down with the lamb. The fox would sleep with the rabbit. The chaos we live in now did not exist at creation. The Bible says that perfect love casts out fear. The emotions like fear, doubt, and unbelief could not enter in because there was perfect love. However, man opened the door to those things when he disobeyed God. Adam and Eve were driven out from the garden into an imperfect world. Soon, brother would rise up against brother and slay him. We sometimes look at our society as being evil, and for the most part it is. What we should not do is blame God. God gave man a choice from creation. Everything in this garden is yours . . . except. Sometimes we take our eyes off of everything we have and look at the . . . *except*. I could do this for God . . . *except*. I could be successful . . . *except*. God will give you everything you need: no EXCEPTIONS.

When man fell, sin entered in. In the garden, the rabbit and lamb had no natural enemy. They did not need to teach the little ewe to be watchful because the lion roamed at night. Likewise, man was also in balance. Adam and Eve did not lie awake at night listening for the sounds of danger. That was something foreign to them, but it all changed when their adversary arrived. Their disobedience changed the course of man. It affected Adam and Eve and all of their descendants, which now affects you and me.

I want to talk to you about something I call a distracted soldier. The Bible calls the Devil an accuser, but make no mistake—he is our Enemy. He knows his target . . . *you*. We are all different but the same. We all have weaknesses, and we all have wounds inflicted by man. He studies us and attacks where we are weak, where our defenses are lacking. Because of this, like it or not, you must become a soldier. This might sound ridiculous, but let me ask you this question in all seriousness. How would a highly trained Navy SEAL fare in battle if he only took a rock to guard himself? He would not survive, right? No one would ever expect a soldier to enter the battlefield without everything he or she needed, but that is exactly what you and I do every day.

The Bible tells us to fully equip ourselves for battle. God has equipped us with everything we need, yet we go into battle time and time again not prepared and become easy prey for the Enemy. The mistake we make is we think we can train at our leisure or prepare on our schedule, but it doesn't work that way. Satan will not wait to attack until you're prepared and fully trained. The battle will come to you when you least expect it. When your adversary comes against you, there will not be time to train, to test out the equipment. When the battle finds you, you must fight with all your might. The problem is, we blame God when we are not ready. You must think of yourself as a soldier. You are about to climb aboard the helicopter that will take you into battle. Are you ready? If not, whom do you blame? I want to make one thing clear: you are a soldier and you are either headed to battle, currently engaging the enemy, or returning from battle. Some of you reading this may have been decimated by the Enemy. You came off the battlefield bruised and broken. I want you to understand that it's okay to crawl off the battlefield, because you can't fight alone. You thought you could handle the situation, but it quickly spiraled out of control. The Devil will make you believe you are in control, and he will lead you to the edge. Once there, he will push you over and all control is gone. The past is gone; you can't change it, but the battles left to face are within your control. When we submit to God, He not only equips us to fight but also leads us when the battle gets hot. Similarly, when you admit to yourself you need help, you're on the road to victory. It's a start, but *only* a start. Picture yourself on the battlefield with the ones you love the most. You take up positions to defend the areas that are vulnerable. The battle begins, but you become distracted, let's say by _____ (you fill in the blank). You know what your distraction is. The problem is, you no longer cover the area that is vulnerable in your life. That not only puts you at risk but also those who are in battle with you . . . your family. This battle thing is a team effort.

Satan wants to distract you and keep you from learning how to win. This is a life battle. You as a victim will view life differently than anyone else. Life has wounded you. You look at life through a different lens than someone who has never felt the pain of abuse or addiction. Learning to recognize the Devil's tactics will help better prepare you so you are not caught off guard. Remember, Satan has weaknesses too. He is not scared of you. He's scared of the one who lives inside you. A made-up mind drives him mad. No matter what he throws at you, it does not move you. You are no longer the victim. You are the VICTOR.

SPIRIT OF OFFENSE

"Great peace have they which love thy law:
and nothing shall offend them."
—Psalm 119:165

Once you make the decision to live for the Lord, I wish I could tell you that life is smooth sailing from that moment on. Unfortunately, it is not. The Enemy takes notice of your decision and does his best—again, from that moment on—to derail you with fear, doubt, and discouragement. He will use offense to destroy your faith. There are so many times we put our faith more in people than we do God, and this is dangerous. People are just that, people. No matter who they are and what position they hold, they are human. They are flawed at the very best and should never be held to the same standard as Christ. This one thing has destroyed many of the people I know. Offense is one of Satan's greatest weapons. If it is not quickly given to God and dealt with, it will eat at your spirit as a cancer and destroy you.

I have had to deal with this in my own life. I can tell you that this can be harder to overcome than alcohol or drug addiction because you can hide it and act like all is well while your spirit is being destroyed little by little. You can be offended and still love God, but don't fool yourself into believing it won't eventually affect your walk with God. You can think you are okay with a person or a situation to find yourself in a moment being flooded with feelings you can't control. It will become as plaque in the artery of your heart. It will build up little by little, over time, until you have a spiritual heart attack and find yourself not being able to feel the presence of God like you are accustomed to or being able to operate freely in His Spirit. When we hold grudges, unforgiveness, or ill feelings against our fellow man, we begin to slowly cut off the free flow of the Spirit in our lives and find ourselves spiritually dry and barren. Isolation will become your greatest defense, and you will find yourself building up walls to protect yourself. But know that the walls you built to protect yourself will ultimately be the walls that prevent you from freely feeling the presence of God. I want to shed light into your soul so you can find freedom and deliverance from the very thing that was sent for your destruction.

When the military goes out on a mission to destroy its target, it does not do so without studying the patterns and movements of its enemy. We should not operate any differently in the Spirit. Satan is out to destroy us. We must wise up, put on the full armor of God, so that we may withstand the attacks of our adversary in these last days. Study the Scriptures and gain an understanding of the ways of the Enemy so that you become knowledgeable of the tactics he will ultimately use against you. When you have dealt with hurt in your life (over and over again, to where it is normal), it is very easy to find yourself putting up walls to protect yourself, but DON'T. What you think is protecting you is actually destroying you. This is why I feel that offense is one of the greatest and subtle attacks that Satan utilizes.

Are you dealing with something? Has someone hurt you or offended you? If so, be honest with yourself; deal with the pain and overcome. You are too valuable to the kingdom of God to allow the Devil to destroy you. You cannot allow yourself to justify your ill feelings. If you begin to justify your anger, bitterness, resentment, jealousy, and even your un-forgiveness, you've put yourself on a dangerous path. If you find yourself doing this, pray that God will help you see yourself as He sees you and open your eyes to realize your true condition so that you may be able to find healing. You cannot begin to heal while you are still blaming everyone else for your feelings.

As God reveals your true condition to you, don't make excuses but immediately find a place of repentance in your life and know that as you embrace your feelings, God will give you strength to overcome. One of the darkest times in my life was when I finally dealt with the spirit of offense. I became a mental, physical, and spiritual mess. I knew that the feelings I felt were not good, and after seeing offense destroy so many that I loved in my life, I knew that I had to deal with this or I would fall victim to it as well.

One Saturday in particular, I found myself crying and praying all day. When I say "all day," I mean *all* day. I found myself being very candid and real with God. The person that had hurt and offended me had no idea they had caused me this much pain. I knew in my heart that if they knew, it would break their heart. Nonetheless, I was still offended and I had to deal with these feelings; they were so strong I knew they would destroy me spiritually. Unfortunately, I found myself regressing and taking on a victim mentality. After I had dealt with so much hurt in my life from people who were supposed to love me the most, it was easy to adopt this mindset once again. I felt justified. After dealing with years of sexual abuse and a bad marriage of physical and emotional abuse, I thought, *Here we go again: someone else I love and respect is letting me down.* We need to be careful of the unrealistic expectations we set for people we love. Don't ever forget that they're human. They are just like you and me. How many times have we hurt someone by our actions or words spoken unintentionally? That's a sobering thought. After dealing with all of the hurt I have experienced in my life, I cannot imagine inflicting that same pain on someone else. Sometimes we hold others to a higher standard than we do ourselves.

As I sat there on my front porch, crying, feeling sorry for myself, justifying every feeling I felt, it was as if the Lord opened my eyes to see myself in this pitiful state. While feeling sorry for myself, a revelation came to me that I had to encourage myself in the Lord just as David did. There was no one around that could make me feel better. I cried out to the Lord in anger and sorrow, asking Him, "Why? Why did this person do this to me? Don't they love me? Don't they realize the hurt that they have caused me?" And I realized that, in reality, they did not. I had allowed my mind to take a few things people had said to me, accompanied by a few actions that I saw, to form a conclusion that may or may not have been accurate.

"For though we walk in the flesh, we do not war after the flesh: (For the weapons of our warfare are not carnal, but mighty through God to the pulling down of strongholds;) Casting down imaginations, and every high thing that exalteth itself against the knowledge of God, and bringing into captivity every thought to the obedience of Christ" (2 Cor. 10:3–5).

Every thought we think is not true. Sometimes the accuser will drop a thought in your mind and then allow you to run with it. With some of us, Satan's job is not very hard at all. All he has to do is plant a thought in our minds, and before you know it we have formed a whole case against a person that may or may not exist. As God began to open my eyes to the realization of my pitiful state, I begin to cry out to Him in repentance, asking for forgiveness. As hard as it was, I began to pray for the person who offended me. I began to pray blessings on them. I told God that I could not do this on my own. If He did not help me overcome these feelings, I was afraid they would destroy me. I would love to tell you healing happened immediately, at that very moment of prayer, but it didn't. I began to pray every day, several times a day, in fact, that God would help me overcome these feelings and love this person as He loved me. That is a hard prayer to pray when the person's actions do not change. But every time I began to feel those feelings come upon me, I began to pray for God to give me strength and wisdom to handle myself as He would desire and to help me love as He loves.

Self-control and discipline became my friend as I began to guard my mind against those thoughts that did not glorify God. I began to realize that God sometimes allows certain trials to come into our lives, not to destroy us, but to perfect us. For God to "use" us, we must go through a purification process to remove all characteristics that are not Christlike. We say with our lips that we want to be like Jesus, but when the trials come to perfect us and shed light on areas of our life that need growth, how will we react? How we react will determine our direction in God. I promise you that if you have dealt with a life of hurt and abuse, you are going to battle a victim mentality. But there is freedom from that mindset. You can overcome. You are not in this battle alone. When you commit your life to God and are filled with His Spirit, you are no longer traveling this road alone. He has given you His Spirit living inside of you to overcome every situation and trial that is sent your way. You just have to overcome the biggest battle, and that is in your mind. You cannot allow yourself to become isolated and alone. When you feel these feelings come your way, you must find a place of prayer, get in touch with God, and immediately surrender those feelings to Him. Do not give credence to the thoughts that the Enemy will place in your mind; instead, give those thoughts to God. This is the only way to win. You must surrender your life to God, pick up the cross, and follow Him daily—in some cases, moment by moment.

Do you want to find true freedom and live a life of deliverance? Then surrender everything to Him and let Him make you anew. The key to overcoming offense is self-honesty. If you realize your true condition and turn it over to God, His Spirit will breathe strength, wisdom, and love into your heart. Don't allow pride to hold you back from surrendering to the Lord and intentionally forgiving those who have hurt you knowingly or unknowingly. Remember that this act is not for them; it is for your healing and spiritual well-being.

STEPS TO FORGIVENESS

"The spirit of a man will sustain his infirmity;
but a wounded spirit who can bear?"
—PROVERBS 18:14

I'm not talking about getting your feelings hurt. I am talking about something that hurts you to the core. When you deal with the deep pain of abuse, rejection, and shame, it changes you emotionally and spiritually. The man who does not have a relationship with God begins to dump hatred on his pain so he doesn't feel it. This same principle applies to violence and revenge as well. Remember: hurt people hurt people. Another tool we use is denial. We do not want to face what hurts us or others. Many of us deal with pain by building walls. But when you build up walls to protect you, they turn into walls that block the flow of God's Spirit. You are no longer a channel God can freely flow through to minister to yourself and others.

How can I be free? Forgiveness. Ask God to heal you, to alleviate your sins, and cleanse you. Though you will not be without faults, and it might take once, twice, or a hundred redemptions, there is only one salvation. That one time you ask for forgiveness could break the wall, letting God rush in to help you. Forgiving yourself is second to asking God for forgiveness. After we seek forgiveness from God, we can begin to bestow that same forgiveness and understanding to others. Forgiveness from God plants the seed of empathy for those in need.

One of the most profound messages on forgiveness I have ever heard was delivered by David Shatwell, a pastor from Oklahoma. It was titled "The Tragedy of a Wounded Spirit." I believe these God-given principles will help anyone who is struggling in the area of forgiveness. I have laid them out in four steps. I want you to implement them immediately if you are dealing with forgiveness issues. I pray this message is as life changing for you as it was for me.

Step One

Describe to God in detail what happened to you. People tend to fear doing this for fear of being overwhelmed by the pain.

You won't have to think hard. The moment will emerge almost immediately. When you do this, don't be surprised how the hurt will resurface and the pain will become real, as if it happened yesterday. Bring out every minute detail. Concentrate on how it made you feel. Don't stop when it gets painful. It's just you and God. Then say, "Lord Jesus, whatever that man or woman did, I forgive and release this person, and I give this hurt and resentment into your hands. I take it and release it back to you." As you say these words,

I want you to take both of your hands and pretend you are grabbing something that's attached to your chest. Grab it and pull it out of your chest, then open your hands to release it to God. There is safety in Christ.

Step Two

"And they stoned Stephen, calling upon God, and saying, 'Lord Jesus, receive my spirit.' And he kneeled down, and cried with a loud voice, 'Lord, lay not this sin to their charge.' And when he had said this, he fell asleep" (Acts 7:59–60).

Stephen was being stoned for the name of Jesus. When he cried out, he didn't say, "Lord, I forgive them." He was saying, "I've already done that, Lord, now it's your turn. I want you to forgive them."

It's one thing to say "I forgive them," but its another thing to ask God to forgive them. We find comfort in our minds thinking that one day, God will take care of them for what they have done to us. But Stephen was saying, "Never lay this charge against them. I don't want them to pay for what they did to me." How will you phrase it? *Lord, never make them pay for the damage they did to my childhood* (or whatever the pain is; you fill in the blank). *The pain they brought upon my life, remember it no more.*

Now ask God to forgive them for what they did to you and never make them pay for the wrong they caused. Tell God that if He needs a witness in judgment, "Do not call me. I refuse to confirm their sin." This step is harder than the first because you are releasing any kind of motive to make them pay for what they did to you. Any thoughts of revenge must be discarded. Think about Jesus on the cross when He said, "Father, forgive them for they know not what they do." Jesus suffered the cross by the hands of cruel, mocking people and still had the strength to see past their injustice. Simply say, "Jesus, as of this day, I have forgiven them. I am asking you to forgive them and never make them pay for the wounds and hurt they have caused me."

Forgiveness is not about them anyway. It's about you and your freedom. It's your future. Remember, you are the one holding up a wall to this person because you are in pain. Does hatred and the need for revenge stop you from healing? Maybe there is also a part of you that feels holding this grudge is causing them pain too. This is never true. Remember not to cast the first stone.

Step Three

When you see the hurt and sin you have caused yourself and others, you must forgive the resentment you hold against yourself. If you are full of resentment, how can you fulfill the Scripture that says, "Love your neighbor as yourself"? (Mark 12:31). If you do not love yourself and have peace with your past, there is little chance you can forgive. After asking God for forgiveness, do not forget to release yourself. Say, "Jesus, I know you have forgiven me for the hurt I have caused others, and from this moment on, I forgive myself. I release myself from all guilt, shame, and resentment."

Step Four

The last step is almost never done. Sometimes, people do not have grudges with other people. They hold them against a specific idea or principle. Most commonly, people have resentment against God. When you do everything you can to live right for the Lord and tragedy comes your way, whether it is abuse or just life's pain, it leaves you asking, "Where are you God?" Consider the story of a young woman with a history of sexual abuse. She is perfect on the outside—attractive, friendly, a straight-A student, and a hard worker. Nobody can tell or guess she has been through tragedy. She is a master at hiding. But her choice of relationships reflect her inner pain. Choosing to flee with abusive or toxic men, she finds herself hiding once more through drugs and alcohol. She begins to fray. Her health spirals down to the point of a well-needed liver transplant, which she cannot afford due to her drug addiction. Her anger toward her abusers and a life filled with abuse and sickness begins to veer over to bigger powers. A loving, caring God could have stopped this, but chose not to. You must understand it is not God's will that any of us endure pain, but by man's sin, pain entered the world and, unfortunately, into our lives. We must let God off the hook and understand sin for what it is—the choice of man.

"A merry heart doeth good like a medicine: but a broken spirit drieth the bones" (Prov. 17:22).

******

A broken spirit. When we read this Scripture, we must understand that it is talking about the spirit of man. It's pointing out that part of you that makes you who you are; your soul, some call it. When your soul or your spirit is broken, the core of who you are is shattered. That part of you that fuels your emotions, your actions, and your decisions is sick. If your soul is sick, every part of you will dry up. Every reservoir in your life will begin to leak. Happiness that fills your heart will begin to elude your grasp, escaping through the cracks of your broken soul.

But that isn't the end of the story. You see, brokenness on your own will kill you, but brokenness in the hands of God will bring you life. If there is anyone in the Bible who knows what loneliness and brokenness is, it is David. David knew what it was to have a broken spirit, and from that place of brokenness, David writes this, "The sacrifices of God are a broken spirit: a broken and a contrite heart, O God, thou wilt not despise" (Ps. 51:17).

You see, your brokenness is not what is killing you; it is your brokenness in your own hands that is doing the job. Although it may seem ironic, your brokenness is not your enemy; it is your friend. Brokenness takes us to Jesus. He wants your brokenness. He wants to take the shattered and despised vessel that you are, place you on His potter's wheel, and begin to put you back together again for His glory, for it "seemed good to the potter to make it" (Jer. 18:4).

The cracks that once told a story of your brokenness will remain as scars, testifying to your healing. What was once ugly will become beautiful. What was once despised will become embraced. Where you couldn't hold anything in—no joy, no love, no happiness; all seeming elusive, seeping from the cracks of your heart just as soon as they came in—God will give you the ability again to retain His blessings. He will fill the cracks; He will heal the wounds. What the Devil has stolen from you, God will restore. Depleted no longer, God will bring you to a place where you will say in the same manner as the psalmist David, "My cup runneth over" (Ps. 23:5).

A MOMENT OF REFLECTION

QUESTIONS

- Am I a distracted soldier? If so, what is my distraction?

_____

_____

_____

- Am I holding on to an offense? If so, what?

_____

_____

_____

- Is there someone I need to forgive?

_____

_____

_____

- What resentments do I hold against myself?

_____

_____

_____

- Am I holding any unforgiveness or resentment against God? If so, why?

_____

_____

_____

10

WHY ME? REVEALED

Have you ever wanted a change but found yourself repeating the same actions over and over again, expecting a different result? I have. It's crazy. In fact, this is the definition of insanity. When you are on the outside of a situation looking in, the solution is always much clearer than it is when you are the one in the middle. There is no dust stirred up in the air, convoluting your vision, impairing your judgment. I remember vividly the moment when I came to myself as the prodigal son did, my eyes being opened to the mess I had made of my life. I was embarrassed and ashamed. I felt I had lost it all and could never regain the ground or respect I had squandered. It's funny, looking back, how I let the Devil mess with my mind. If he can defeat you in your mind, he has won.

Honestly, I think we give the Devil too much credit. We are our own worst enemy. One of the Devil's tricks is to flood your mind with fear. You fear getting hurt (or hurt again), the loss of income, the loss of health, the loss of a loved one, what people think of you, death . . . the list goes on and on. You become a prisoner of your own making and find yourself wandering aimlessly through life. You're too scared to make a change, so you let the guilt of *not* changing weigh you down. Failure and fear destroys your self-confidence, affects your attitude, your ability to dream, and your direction. You find yourself paralyzed and begin to live a life full of fear and regret. There is a difference between being afraid and fearful. Being fearful paralyzes you. It stops you from moving forward. It keeps you from making a change in your life. Being afraid heightens your senses. You are more in tune with what's happening around you. It's okay to be afraid, but not to live in fear.

Let's look at Job one more time. Here is poor old Job. He was blessed in every way, with not a care in the world. Little did he know the Devil was about to bring his world down. In the span of a few hours, Job lost almost everything. His children, livestock, and servants were all taken from him. We all know the story of Job. But here's something you might not have picked up on. Go back and read the story again. At any point did the Devil tell Job what he was about to do? No. God allowed Satan to touch his children, livestock, and servants, but did not give him permission to kill Job. The Devil continuously tells you what he's about to do to you. "If you try to change, I'll do this" or "Mess with me, and I'll do that." If he's telling you what he's going to do, that means he doesn't have permission. If he did, it would happen. No warning, just action. So the next time the Devil tries to torment your mind with what he's about to do, just grin and say, "Not today, not *ever*."

It is crucial that you have God as the commander of your life and allow Him to order your steps. As a soldier in battle, it is imperative for you to know your enemy—their location and tactics— so you can defeat them. No soldier goes into battle without knowing his opponent. How can you gain this understanding? Read the Bible. It is your blueprint for life. There is story after story of how the children of God engaged in battle. But they did not win a single victory based on their own abilities. Instead, they depended on the Lord and allowed Him to fight their battles. Why do you study history? Because if you can learn from others' mistakes and not repeat them, you have hope in changing your world one life at a time, starting with your own. The Devil doesn't want you to get this. Trust me. If you can grasp this one concept, it is a huge blow to his kingdom. If the enemy of your soul can keep you so consumed with fear and worry of the "what-ifs" in life, you will never take a chance and change.

There is freedom in understanding this concept. Life is a gift. But how many times have you seen lives—including your own—that have been wasted by fear and worry?

You must let go and let God have control. You must seek the face of God and pursue your purpose like never before. The Bible says in Proverbs 29:18, "Where there is no vision, the people perish ..." When you have a purpose or a mission and you know what you want, nothing can stop you. When you lack direction and purpose, you find yourself just wandering through life, being controlled by others and their plans rather than your own. God gave you a purpose, so find it and pursue it with all your might. You cannot do this task alone. You need the Lord. Plug into the power source and don't let your weaknesses or sense of inadequacies control you. When you do this, you will find His strength and power kick in when yours becomes weak.

Paul says in 2 Corinthians 12:9, "And he said unto me, 'My grace is sufficient for thee: for my strength is made perfect in weakness.' Most gladly therefore will I rather glory in my infirmities, that the power of Christ may rest upon me."

You must realize you cannot control everything and everyone. You must accept this as reality. Release those things to God you can't control, and trust in Him to work everything for your good as the Scriptures state. When you focus on God, your mindset, actions, and spirituality will all fall into place. There is so much freedom in this concept that when you start implementing it, you will begin living all over again. I mean TRUE living, not just merely existing. You will find restoration and healing. You will find the things you thought you had lost being restored, such as your integrity. People will begin to trust you and, most importantly, you will begin to trust *yourself*. Your confidence and ability to move forward will be strong because you have let go of control and put God as commander of your life. Trust is powerful. It's the foundation of any relationship. Without trust, you have nothing. The decision you have made to give your life to God and pursue His perfect plan is not a small one that you should overlook. The decisions you make determine your destiny, and you are definitely on the right track.

My pastor D. G. Hargrove says this often: "What we value will determine our desires. Our desires will establish our priorities. Our priorities will set our direction. Our direction will determine our destiny."

Now, become a student of His Word, and make up your mind that you want everything God has for you.

We have talked about many things in this book, and I pray my experiences and hard- learned life lessons will help you begin the healing process. I want you to continue on the road to healing, pursuing your purpose with a vengeance.

We were all created for a purpose, and I encourage you to seek God. He will reveal your destiny to you. Don't overcomplicate the will of God. It's simple. He wants a relationship with you. Commit to a life of prayer, reading His Word and living a holy life. Leave the details to Him. God won't let you down.

It's amazing how when your relationship with God is healthy, you are able to have healthy relationships. When you try to operate in opposition to this principle, selfishness arises and distorts your view. It inevitably destroys relationships. I would love to tell you what your purpose is, because I know how priceless that can be, but that is something you must find for yourself.

What I will tell you is this: when I stopped seeking purpose and started seeking God, things began to shift and doors began to open.

When you find healing, your mission is not complete. You have found healing for a purpose. What will you do with it? Share your testimony and watch God work. Your testimony will be an inspiration to others to change and pursue God like never before.

"And they overcame him by the blood of the Lamb, and by the word of their testimony; and they loved not their lives unto the death" (Rev. 12:11).

So, "why me?" Jesus Christ Himself, while praying in the Garden of Gethsemane, asked this question too. In His humanity, He couldn't bear the thought of the pain on the cross. He couldn't bear to think about the embarrassment of being nailed to a tree, exposed and naked, before those whom He loved, gasping for breath as life drained from His body. In His humanity, He could not bear the thought. That night, overcome with anxiety, fear, and loneliness, He prayed so hard that He even sweat His own blood. But in the middle of His prayer of despair, there was a shift in His attitude. From uttering the words, "O my Father, if it be possible, let this cup pass from me," Jesus' words began to shift, His tone began to change, His anxiety began to settle, and His heartbeat began to regulate. He then uttered these words as time stood still, eternity stood at attention, and the destiny of humanity hung in the balance, "Nevertheless, not as I will, but as thou will" (Matt. 26:39).

Many times I have read this thinking, what changed? Why the sudden shift in His demeanor and attitude? Did He give up? No. He did not give up. In fact, He did quite the opposite; He gave in. Because in that very moment, praying a prayer for Himself, Jesus Christ looked up and saw you: two thousand years in the making, He saw you. He saw you in your brokenness. He saw you in your pain. He saw you in your loneliness. He saw you in your hurt. He saw you crying for help, and when He saw YOU, He saw His purpose. To Him, the purpose of your healing was far greater than His pain. Your restoration was far greater than stripes on His back, the thorns in His head, the nails in His hands and feet, or a spear in His side. He said "nevertheless" because He saw YOU. That is how much Jesus loves you and is willing to see you healed.

So the next time that you ask yourself, or even God, "why me?" know that you are not alone. Know that He understands just where you are. Know that He is empathetic to the pain in your moment of despair, but even in the middle of your despair, He is beckoning you to look up. For when you look up, you just might see the answer to your question, *Why me?*

A MOMENT OF REFLECTION

QUESTIONS

- How am I my own worst enemy?

_____

_____

- How have I allowed fear to paralyze me?

_____

_____

- Has worry become my companion? If so, how?

_____

_____

- What things must I relinquish control of and give to God?

_____

_____

- What steps can I take to live life more intentionally and purpose driven?

_____

_____

- How can I better impact my world?

_____

_____

MY PRAYER FOR YOU

In the name of Jesus, I speak healing and restoration into every life. I pray that the Spirit of God will break every yoke, chain of addiction, and sin. May God breathe life into the depths of your soul. I pray that God will grant you the courage to remove your mask and allow Him into those secret places that no one goes. Lord, I pray that you will reveal yourself to them in a powerful way. Let them feel and sense your presence like never before. I pray you guide them and give them strength and courage to take every burden and care to the cross of Calvary, never to be picked up again. I pray they will no longer live under the weight of condemnation, but freely accept your love and forgiveness. Let their sight be opened so they can see themselves as you see them. Allow them to comprehend their own personal value as well as their value to your kingdom. Let them feel your unconditional love. Reveal yourself to them in a greater dimension. I pray from this moment forth that each and every person will rise up with boldness and courage, declaring, "I am more than a conqueror in Christ Jesus." I speak freedom into their spirit, freedom from all guilt, shame, and condemnation from past abuse. Put their shame from poor choices under your blood. Lord, I pray you give them the strength to rise above their critics and be the man or woman of God you have called them to be. I pray that your Spirit fills the room where they are sitting. I ask that whatever bondage holds them down be removed. Break down every wall that keeps them in prison. Lord, I pray from this day forth you will empower them with your Spirit to rise up and live in total freedom. I pray you would guide their footsteps and lead them on this journey of healing. Let their lives never be the same again. By faith, I thank you in advance for complete healing and restoration in every life so that each person can rise up and live out their God-given destiny. In Jesus' name I pray. Amen.

THE GIFT OF MUSIC

Take a moment and visit www.whymebook.com and listen to "Why Me." "Why Me" was written and recorded by my son, Justin Michael, to accompany the ministry of this book.

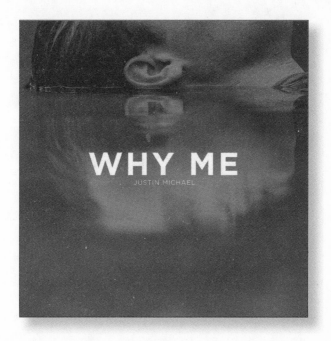

CONTACT THE AUTHOR

Please email your testimony or examples of how this book may have helped you. I would love to hear from you and learn about what God is doing in your life.

To contact the author or to book speaking engagements:
Misty Michael
Local: 214-989-4130
Toll Free: 855-944-4949
Email: misty@whymebook.com
Web: whymebook.com

Visit whymebook.com
Subscribe to my blog for updated posts, as I discuss real issues that affect our daily walk with God. I pray that you will find healing through God's Word.

NOTES

NOTES